PLAYING WITH

Lucy Sanctuary

Published by

Speechmark Publishing Ltd, Sunningdale House, 43 Caldecotte Lake Drive,
Milton Keynes MK7 8LF, United Kingdom
Tel: +44 (0)1908 277177   Fax: +44 (0)1908 278297
www.speechmark.net

Designed by Moo Creative (Luton)

002-5893 - Printed in the United Kingdom by CMP (uk) Ltd

British Library Cataloguing in Publication Data
A catalogue record for this book is available from the British Library.

ISBN: 978 0 86388 964 6

CONTENTS

ACKNOWLEDGEMENTS

I would like to thank:

Jo Gilmore for her support and advice, for being an amazing speech and language therapist and an even more amazing friend;

Sarah Norman and Judy Avery, for their encouragement and support;

Frances and Claire Burnham, Una Kroll and Tracey Fricker for putting up with me throughout the writing of this book;

Hilary and Stephanie for giving me this opportunity;

all the children who have played these games and enabled me to write this book.

This book is dedicated to my children, Phoebe and Felix Sanctuary, for tolerating the ups and downs of writing this book!

Many thanks to my mother, Maureen Baylis, for her endless support.

INTRODUCTION

Why do some children need support to use speech sounds?

Children usually start saying single words by 12 months (Flynn & Lancaster, 1996). By four and a half years, most children can use nearly all of the 24 consonant speech sounds that are in the English language, for example **m, b, p, s, k**. These speech sounds follow a developmental order: most children start saying the speech sounds **m, n, b, p, t, d, w** between 18 months and two years of age (Grunwell, 1985).

The development of speech sounds in children's talking.

One and half years old to two years old	m, n, p, b, t, d, w
Two years old to two and a half years old	m, n, p, b, t, d, w Some children start saying h, k, g and ng (as in ing). These sounds are made at the back of the mouth.
Two and a half years old to three years old	m, n, p, b, t, d, w, h, k, g, ng, f, s, y Some children start to say l.
Three years old to three and a half years old	m, n, p, b, t, d, w, h, k, g, ng, f, s, y, l. Some children start to say ch and sh.
Three and a half years old to four and a half years old	m, n, p, b, t, d, w, h, k, g, ng, f, s, z, y, l, sh, ch, j. Some children start to say r.

Source: Grunwell, 1985

However, not all children acquire the consonant speech sounds in the typical order of development. For example, some children need help to say a group of speech sounds called fricatives, such as **s, z, f, v**. These are long speech sounds, as opposed to short speech sounds such as **t** and **d**. Children who are following the typical development path acquire short speech sounds, such as **t** and **d**, **k** and **g**, before they acquire long speech sounds such as **s** and **f**. We make long speech sounds (fricatives) by pushing air through a restricted space in our mouths.

For example, when we say the speech sound **s**, the tongue is at the top of the mouth behind the top teeth. It restricts the airflow coming out of the mouth by leaving a small space between the tongue and the roof of the mouth for the air to pass through, which makes a hissy sound. Some children find it easier to say short speech sounds, for example **t** instead of **s**, **d** instead of **z**. This is called *stopping*. Most children say the speech sounds **s** and **f** in their talking between the ages of three and three and a half whereas most children say the speech sounds **t** and **d** in their talking between the ages of one and a half and two (Grunwell, 1985).

There are various reasons why some children need support to use speech sounds. Listed below are some factors that can affect the development of speech sounds:

- Hearing impairments.

- Some children have frequent colds and ear infections such as glue ear which can make it difficult for them to hear speech sounds accurately. We need to be able to hear a speech sound clearly in order to copy it and say it accurately. Difficulties hearing a speech sound can result in difficulties saying it.

- Attention and listening difficulties and short concentration spans can result in difficulties hearing speech sounds accurately. Children with these difficulties often miss important visual information about how we say speech sounds, for example the shape of our lips, where we put the tongue. This can affect the child's ability to say speech sounds correctly.

- Some children develop more slowly than others and need more time to use speech sounds (developmental delay).

- Children need to hear people talking in order to learn how to use speech sounds. Lack of opportunities to hear speech can affect the development of speech sounds.

- Using a dummy or sucking a bottle until two and a half or three can restrict the range of tongue movements a child makes, and this can affect their speech. For example, some children who use a dummy for a long time say the speech sounds **k** and **g**, which are made at the back of the mouth, instead of the speech sounds **t** and **d**, which are made at the front of the mouth. This is because the dummy restricts movement of the tongue tip, which we use to say the speech sounds **t** and **d**.

- Some children have difficulty coordinating the movements needed for speech, for example tongue movements, lip movements, breath support, because they have speech disorders or developmental verbal dyspraxia (DVD). Developmental verbal dyspraxia 'is a condition where the child has difficulty in making and co-ordinating the precise movements which are used in the production of spoken language, although there is no damage to muscles or nerves' (Ripley *et al.*,1997). The child knows what they want to tell you, but difficulties coordinating the precise movements needed to say it, for example sequencing tongue movements and lip movements, can make it very hard for listeners to understand what the child wants to tell them. In other words, what the child says does not match what they want to say. 'My mouth won't co-operate with my brain' (quote from Kevin, aged 13 in Stackhouse, 1992).

- Speech sound difficulties are often found in families, so there may be other family members who have had help to say speech sounds accurately.

How does difficulty using speech sounds affect children?

Children with speech sound difficulties are often hard for people outside the family to understand. Children can become reluctant to talk as they are worried that others will not understand what they want to say. Speech sound difficulties can prevent a child from taking part in nursery and classroom activities and limit their ability to express themselves – to ask questions, to give opinions, to tell stories, etc. Children often worry that, if they put their hand up to answer a question, no one will understand what they say and other children may laugh at them. Communication difficulties can lead to low self-confidence and low self-esteem.

The speech sound s

You may like to know that:

- Most children start to say the speech sound **s** at around three to three and a half years of age (Grunwell, 1985).

- We make the speech sound **s** at the front of our mouths, by lifting the tongue so that it is close to the top of the mouth, behind the top teeth.

- The tongue is not blocking the air from coming out of the mouth, but it restricts the space that the air has to come out. The air is forced out of a small space, which makes **s** sound hissy. Say **sea** and feel the tongue lift towards the roof of your mouth, behind your top teeth. If you put your hand in front of your mouth when you say **sea** you can feel the air released down the middle of your tongue. This can help children to say **s**.

- The tongue touches the top teeth at the sides of the mouth when we say **s**. Say **s** and feel your top teeth touching the sides of your tongue.

- The speech sound **s** is a quiet sound, not a noisy speech sound like **z**.

- The speech sound **s** is a long sound, not a short speech sound like **t**.

- The speech sound (phoneme) **s** is not the same as the letter (grapheme) **s**. When we say the letter **s**, we say **es**.

- When **ce** follows a vowel sound, it is pronounced as the speech sound **s**, for example in words like **ace**, **nice**, **mice**, **juice**, **force**. (NB. the graphemes **or** and **ui** are

pronounced as long vowel sounds, **or** and **oo**.)

- **cy** is pronounced **s** in words, for example **cyst, Lucy, bicycle**.

- The letter **x** is pronounced as **ks**, for example **axe, mix, fox**.

- The letter **s** is not always pronounced as the speech sound **s**.

- When we write **s** after a noisy speech sound (a voiced speech sound), for example **d, g, m, n**, and vowels, we say **z** instead of **s**. To hear the two different pronunciations of the letter **s**, say **pots**. Because **t** is a quiet speech sound, the letter **s** is pronounced as the speech sound **s**. Now say **pods**. Because **d** is a noisy speech sound, the **s** at the end of word is pronounced as the speech sound **z**.

- Children may say **t** instead of **s**, for example they may say **tea** instead of **sea**. The speech sound **t** is made at the front of the mouth, by lifting the tip of the tongue and putting it behind the top teeth to stop the air coming out of the mouth. It blocks the air from being released. When the tongue tip is lowered the air is released, like a small explosion. It is a short speech sound (a plosive). Say **t**. Feel your tongue tip touching the top of your mouth behind your top teeth (this is your alveolar ridge). Most children say the speech sound **t** before they say **s** in their talking.

- Children may say **d** instead of **s**, for example they may say **door** instead of **saw**. We say the speech sounds **t** and **d** in the same place as we say the speech sound **s** (they are alveolar speech sounds). The speech sound **s** is a long sound. The speech sounds **t** and **d** are short speech sounds.

- Some children put their tongue between their teeth when they say the speech sound **s** (interdental production). This sounds like the speech sound **th** (lisp).

- Some children block the air from being released down the middle of the tongue when they say the speech sound **s** by touching the top of the mouth behind the top teeth with the tongue. This pushes the air out of the sides of the mouth, which makes the speech sound **s** sound slushy (alveolar lateral fricative).

About this book

What is it?

Playing with s is a resource for nursery practitioners, teachers, teaching assistants, carers, speech and language therapists and speech and language therapy assistants to use in order to help children to say **s** in their talking. It contains activities, games and ideas to use with children aged from three years old to seven years old. It can also be used with older children who have learning difficulties. Each section contains simple, easy-to-follow instructions and practical tips to help you support the child you are working with. All the materials can be photocopied and instructions are given to help you make the resources for activities. There are progress forms in each section to help you and the child record progress. There are examples of session plans in Section 10 to help you use the resources.

Playing with s aims to:
- give children opportunities to hear **s** in games, activities and jingles
- give children opportunities to practise saying **s** in games, activities and jingles
- provide a clear, easy-to-follow structure for activities
- provide tips to help you support children who have difficulties with certain activities
- be fun!

How long should sessions be?

Keep sessions short and carry them out regularly, perhaps 15 minutes five days a week. Be flexible. For example, if the child is not able to concentrate for 15 minutes, perhaps if they have attention and listening difficulties, make sessions shorter and gradually lengthen them as and when the child is ready. If the child can concentrate for longer, you can increase the length of sessions. Every child is different and this book allows you to tailor sessions to suit the individual. Take sessions in a quiet environment so that the child can focus on the work that you are doing and will not be distracted.

How to use the book

The book is divided into twelve sections. The first seven sections follow the typical acquisition of speech sounds by children:

- Section 1 contains exercises for the mouth (oro-motor exercises). It aims to help children to learn about their mouths and practise movements that can help speech, for example rounding and spreading their lips.
- Section 2 aims to help children say the single speech sound, **s**.
- Section 3 contains short words that begin with the speech sound **s**, such as **sea**, **saw**, **Sue**.
- Section 4 contains longer words that begin with the speech sound **s**, such as **seat**, **sun**, **sock**.
- Section 5 contains words that end with the speech sound **s**, such as **house**, **dance**, **purse**.
- Section 6 contains words that begin or end with **s** and have more than one syllable, such as **seagull**, **sandwich**, **soldier**, **octopus**, **waitress**.
- Section 7 contains words that have the speech sound **s** in the middle of the word, such as **parcel**, **message**, **bicycle**.

Each activity section contains listening and speaking activities. This gives the child opportunities to hear the speech sound and see how to say it before copying it in a speaking activity. For example, round your lips or spread your lips, raise your tongue at the front of the mouth or at the back of the mouth.

Sections 3, 4, 5, 6 and 7 include sets of jingles which use the words that you have been working on with the child. For example:

Sue saw Si,
Si saw Sue,
Sue, **say** hi to **Si**.

At the end of each activity section you will find progress sheets to help you and the child record progress you are making in the sessions and suggestions for what to do next.

- Section 8 provides opportunities to use all the words presented in the book in phrases and sentences in a variety of activities and games.

- Section 9 contains instructions and resources for games which can be played with words from all the sections in the book to provide extra practice. Templates for resources are included with instructions on how to make them.

- Section 10 contains examples of session plans in Section 10 to give you ideas for using this book with children.

- Section 11 contains ideas for working on saying **s** in words and sentences in the nursery, classroom and home.

- Section 12 is a list of the words that are used in each section, including those in the jingles.

This book allows you to be flexible and to follow the needs of the child that you are helping. The amount of time you spend working on each section will depend on the child and the speed of their progress. There are ideas for making the activities more challenging and tips on how to make them easier so that you can tailor what you are doing to suit each individual child.

You will see that Sections 3, 4, 5 and 6 contain some of the same activities, for example 'Listen and guess', 'What's the word?', but using different words in different sections – short words in Section 3 (eg **sea**, **saw**, **sew**), longer words that begin with **s** in Section 4 (eg **safe**, **seal**, **sum**), words that end with **s** in Section 5 (eg **moose**, **rice**, **kiss**) and words that have more than one syllable in Section 6 (eg **sausage**, **cinema**, **saucepan**). The activities have been printed in full in each section (apart from Section 7, which uses activities from all the previous sections) for the following reasons:

- All activities can be photocopied and used alone.

- You do not have to refer back to earlier sections in the book in order to find instructions for activities, although the tips in Section 3 will be helpful in later activities too.

- You can access the book easily at any level. For example, if the child you are working with is having difficulty saying **s** at the end of words, you can start working on Section 5 without having to look back to earlier sections for instructions.

Tip

Photocopy pictures and resources on to card or laminate them for all activities so that you can use them again. Cut out the small pictures of the words you are working on to use in activities and games.

How to help the child to use the speech sound in their everyday talking

Changing the way a child speaks can take time. This can be very frustrating for carers and the child. Using one speech sound instead of another, for example saying **t** in words instead of **s**, can become a habit. In order to change this habit, children need regular opportunities to hear the speech sound they are not yet using, eg **s**, and to practise saying it. Children are often able to use the speech sound they are working on in sessions with support from, for example, a speech therapist or a teaching assistant. However, outside these sessions, they often continue to have difficulty using the speech sound in their talking. This can be demotivating for carers who are working with the child and for the child. Change does not happen overnight and progress can be slow. This is perfectly normal and does not mean the child will never be able to change their talking. Using progress sheets can help you and the child to see changes. Tell older children that it will take time to help them say **s** in their talking and that you will need to work on saying **s** regularly. Photocopy exercises and activities from the book and give them to carers so that they can carry out work with the child at home.

Tips
- Be careful not to overload the child as this can be demotivating. Keep sessions short and fun so that the child remains engaged and interested. Give lots of praise and positive feedback to encourage the child.

- Avoid correcting the child as this can make them feel bad about their talking and it does not help them to change the speech sounds they are using. Instead of correcting the child, repeat what they have said *without the speech sound error* so that the child has an opportunity to hear the word that they want to say but cannot yet say in their talking. For example: if the child says '**Tea**! Look! The **tea**!' you say '**Sea**! Look! The **sea**!' It can help the child if you repeat the word a few times in as natural a context as you can. For example: 'Look at the waves! The **sea** looks cold! I wouldn't swim in the **sea** today! Would you swim in the **sea** today? Look! There's a boat on the **sea**' (four repetitions of sea). This can feel unnatural and be difficult to do, but it is worth trying.

- The jingles at the end of sections give the child more opportunities to hear the words that you are working on. If possible, try reading them at set times such as at bedtime or after dinner. As the jingles become more familiar and the child makes progress with their talking, start leaving pauses for them to complete the jingles (see instructions for using jingles at the end of Section 3).

- Encourage children to think about their talking so that they are actively involved in the speech therapy work. Give them information about speech sounds to help them monitor their talking. For example: 'You said **tea**. **t**, that's a short sound. I said **sea**. **s**, that's a long sound. Listen. **Sea**.' Exaggerate the speech sound **s** at the beginning of sea: **sssssea**, to highlight the fact that it is a long speech sound. This can help children to listen and learn more about the speech sound they actually say and the speech sound they want to say. Often children do not know that they are saying, for example, **t** instead of **s** in words. They need your help and support to realise that what they are saying is not what they want to say. Always model a speech sound or word for children so that they can hear it before they try to say it.

- Raise their awareness by offering them choices. For example: 'Is it **tea** [hold out a fist as you say tea] or is it **sea** [hold out the other fist]?' If the child cannot yet say **s** in words, they can choose between **sea** and **tea** by touching one of your fists, either the fist that you held out when you said **sea**, or the fist that you held out when you said **tea**.

How can I use this resource in the nursery or the classroom?

- Play group or class listening games at carpet time – after registration, before break times, after lunch. You could put one of the resources to help children say **s** on the board, for example 'Put a seal in the sea and say **s**' from Section 2. Choose a child to come to the board. Ask the child to listen and when they hear you say **s**, put a seal in the sea. Count silently to at least four before you say **s** so that the child has to wait. When the child has finished their go, ask them to choose another child to come to the board to listen and put a seal in the sea when they hear **s**. Let the first child say **s** for the second child. The children take it in turns to choose the next child to be the listener and to say **s** in the activity (see listening activities in Section 2).

- See instructions for games using words containing the speech sound **s** in Section 9, for example charades. Play these with the group or class perhaps before lunch or at the end of the day before home time.

- Choose a word of the week from the words you have been working on. Put it on the board and tell the group or class that they have to clap or stand up every time they hear you say the word.

- Choose a picture of one of the words you have been working on, for example **salt**. Describe it to the children: 'It's white. It's very small crystals. It comes from the sea. We put it on food to make it taste better. We use it when we cook. It tastes good on chips! Hands up if you know what it is!' Choose a child to describe the next picture.

- Read at least one jingle from the jingle sections in this book to the group or class. See instructions in Section 3 on ideas for using the jingles.

- Have a jingle of the week and teach the children actions to go with it to make the jingle more memorable and fun!

- Make your own jingles in class using curriculum vocabulary words that contain **s**.

- Start an **s** poster or book in the class. When you work on curriculum topic vocabulary such as mini beasts, habitats, our environment, put words that contain **s** on the poster or in the book (with pictures if possible to make them more visual).

- Play mouth exercise games with the group or class at carpet time or before literacy sessions. See Section 1 of this book for activities, games and pictures.

- Put at least three pictures of words you have been working with on a tray or in a bag.

- Put another three pictures of words that start with a different speech sound on the tray or in the bag, for example **t: tap**, **teddy**, **toe**.

- Ask the children to sort the pictures into ones that start with the speech sound **s** and ones that don't, or ones that start with the speech sound **s** and ones that start with the speech sound **t**.

- Bury pictures in a sand tray. Bury some that start or end with the speech sound **s**, for example **seat**, **sandwich**, **seagull**, and some that start with another speech sound, such as **t: tie**, **tiger**, **tomato**. See if the children can find the pictures that start or end with **s**. A variation is to use a salt timer and see how many pictures they can find in a minute.

- Clap, tap, stamp, drum and count the syllables of words you have been working on, for example **sea – gull** (two syllables).

SECTION 1
EXERCISES FOR THE MOUTH

Section 1: Exercises for the mouth

Aim
To learn about our mouths and practise movements that can help speech.

How?
By giving the child opportunities to see you carry out the exercises and to copy them.

Resources
- A mirror so that the child can watch herself copying the exercises.
- Large pictures of mouth exercises (pp16–27).
- At least two sets of small pictures of mouth exercises (pp28–29). Photocopy the sheet of shapes (p83) on to the back of the pictures so that they are double sided.
- A dice.
- Template for a dice with a different shape on each face (p30).
- A set of the emotions cards, eg *say it in a quiet voice, say it in a loud voice, say it in a sad voice* (p31).

Instructions
1. Put the mirror in front of the child so that you can see yourselves.

   Tell the child that you are going to do some exercises for your mouth! Before you start, ask her, for example, to show you her tongue, show you her teeth, open her mouth wide, give you a big smile. Encourage her to look in the mirror when she does these warm-up movements.

2. Look at the large pictures, read the instruction and demonstrate the movement for the child using the mirror. Then say 'You try!'

NB: the instruction *smile like a granny* means to smile without showing your teeth (spread your lips).

Variations
Keep this activity short and fun. When the child is familiar with the exercises, make them more challenging:

- Carry out the instructions to sequence movements, eg *Can you put your tongue up to your nose and then down to your chin?* Always demonstrate movements for the child before she has a turn so that she can see what you want her to do.

- Take it in turns to roll the dice and carry out the sequence of movements that number of times. For example, if the child throws a 4, she has to move her tongue up and down four times.

- Turn the set of small pictures face down on the table so that you can see the shapes on the back but not the mouth movement. Use the template to make a dice with shapes on the faces. Take it in turns to throw the shape dice at least twice. Turn over the pictures that have those shapes on the back. For example, if you throw a circle, turn over the picture that has a circle on it so that you can see the mouth movement, eg *smile like a granny*. If you throw a star, turn over the picture that has a star on it so that you can see the mouth movement, eg *say ee*. Then throw the number dice to see how many times you have to do the mouth movements. For example: if you throw a 6, you have to *smile like a granny* and then *say ee* six times.

- Put at least two sets of the small pictures face down in front of the child. Take it in turns to turn over two pictures and do the movement on each picture. If the two pictures are the same, for example *blow a kiss* and *blow a kiss*, keep them as a pair. The winner is the person who has the most pairs.

- Photocopy the resource that tells you how to speak, eg *say it in a quiet voice*, *say it in a happy voice*, and cut it into cards. Put them in a pile, face down. Put at least two sets of the small pictures of *say ah, say oo* and *say ee* face down in front of the child. Take it in turns to turn a picture over and take a card from the pile. Carry out the instructions. For example, if the picture is *say oo* and the card is *say it in a loud voice*, you have to say the speech sound **oo** loudly!

- Place a barrier in between you and the child so that you cannot see each other's pictures. Make sure that you both have at least two sets of the small pictures of mouth movements. Choose at least four pictures from your set. For example: *smile like a granny, blow a kiss, say ah, say ee*. Do not show the child. Arrange the pictures behind the barrier so that she cannot see them. The child watches you copy the mouth movements, eg *smile like a granny, blow a kiss, say ah, say ee*, and puts the matching pictures from her set behind the barrier. When she has finished, ask her to show you the mouth movements that are on the pictures she has chosen so that she has a turn at copying the movements. Then remove the barrier to see if she has the same pictures as you. When the child is familiar with this activity, reverse it so that she chooses the pictures and demonstrates them for you.

Tips
- To practise lip movements:
  - Try blowing whistles, blowing kisses, blowing bubbles, blowing musical instruments, whistling!
  - Put on lipstick and kiss a piece of paper – one for the girls perhaps!
  - Fill cheeks with air and then pop (see picture on p26)!

- To practise tongue movements:
  - Try holding a small food item, eg a Cheerio or a Polo on the skin just behind the top teeth (alveolar ridge). Tell the child to push against it as hard as she can with her tongue.

– Gently touch around the child's mouth, eg her chin, one of her cheeks, her nose. The child has to move her tongue to the place you touched.

– Ask the child to put her tongue inside her cheek and push against the cheek. Then you try pushing back against the child's tongue so that she has to push harder (see picture on p27).

My progress

Date	I can ...	☺/☹	I need to work on ...
	Do all of the mouth exercises without any help.		
	Do all of the mouth exercises with some help.		
	Do most of the mouth exercises without any help.		
	Do most of the mouth exercises with some help.		
	Do some of the mouth exercises without any help.		
	Do some of the mouth exercises with some help.		
	Do a few of the mouth exercises without any help.		
	Do a few of the mouth exercises with some help.		

Tip

• Start sessions with a few mouth exercises, even when the child can do all the mouth exercises without any help. The exercises can be used as a warm-up activity before you start working with speech sounds.

can you

smile like a granny

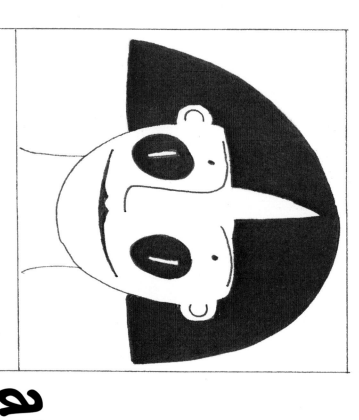

and then

say oo

can you

say ah

and then

smile like a granny

can you put your tongue

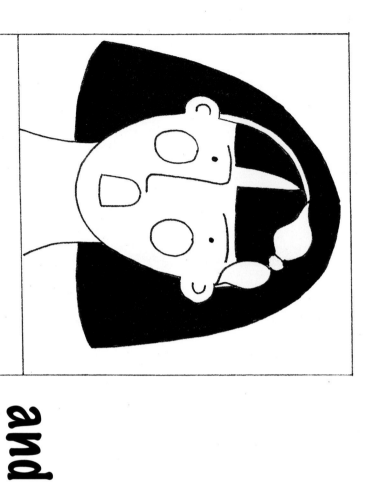

up to your nose

and
then

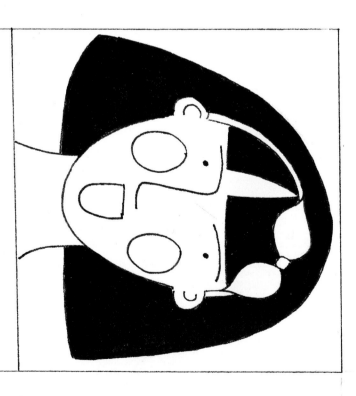

down to your chin

can you

say ah

and
then

say oo

blow a kiss

and then

smile like a granny

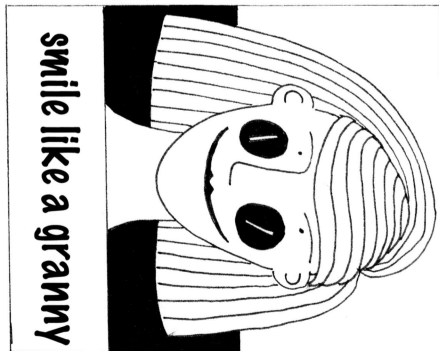

can you say

say ee

and
then

say ah

say ah

and then

say oo

can you

can you put your tongue

right

and then

left

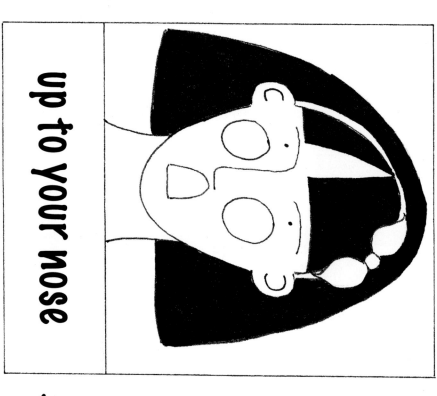

up to your nose

and then

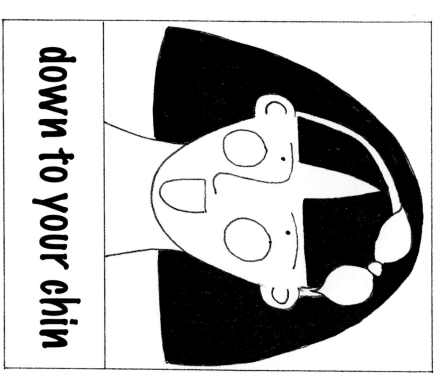

down to your chin

24

can you put your tongue

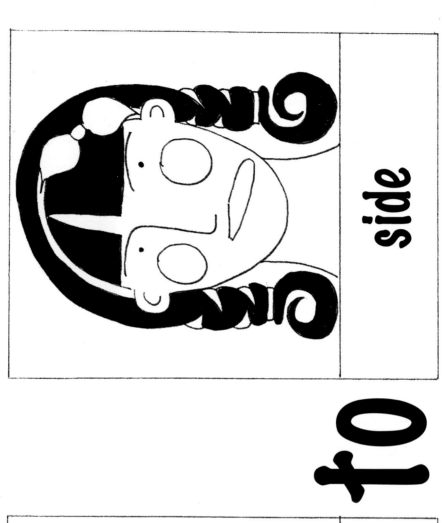

side

to

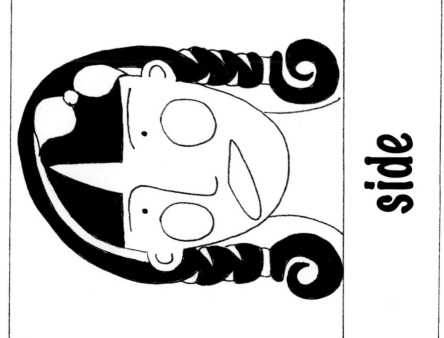

side

25

can you

fill your cheeks with air

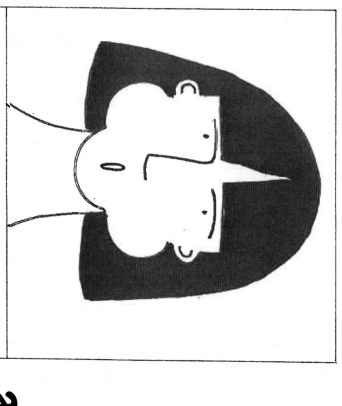

and then

pop your cheeks!

can you

Push against your cheek
with your tongue

and
then

Push against your cheek
with tongue

Fill your cheeks with air

say ah

Push against your cheek with your tongue

say oo

Push against your cheek with your tongue

say ee

28

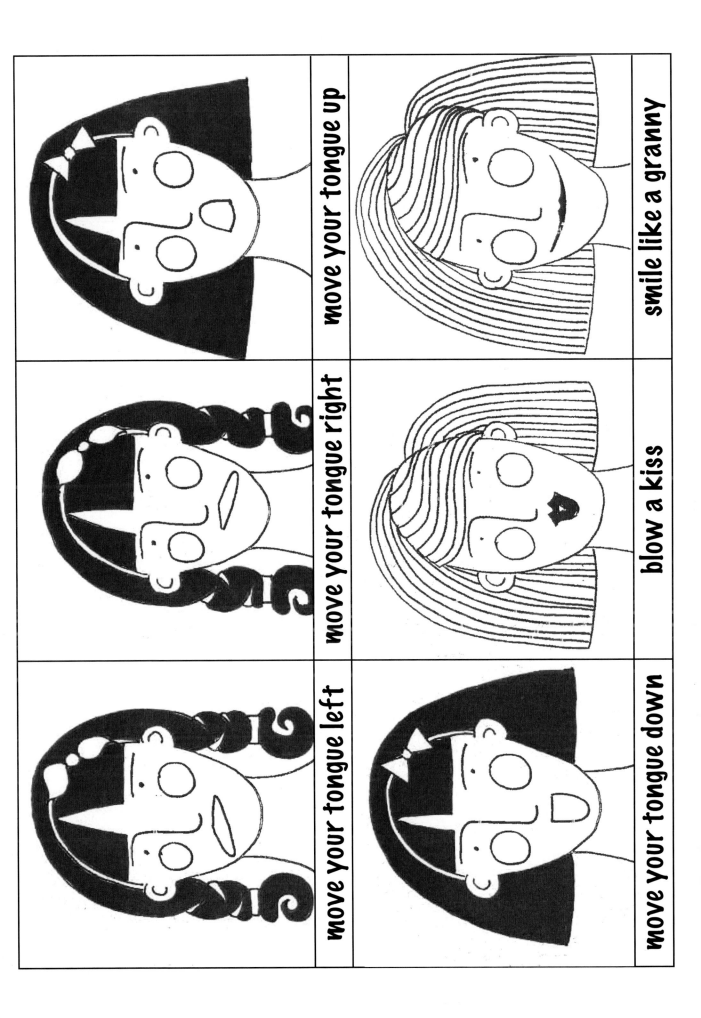

move your tongue up

smile like a granny

move your tongue right

blow a kiss

move your tongue left

move your tongue down

29

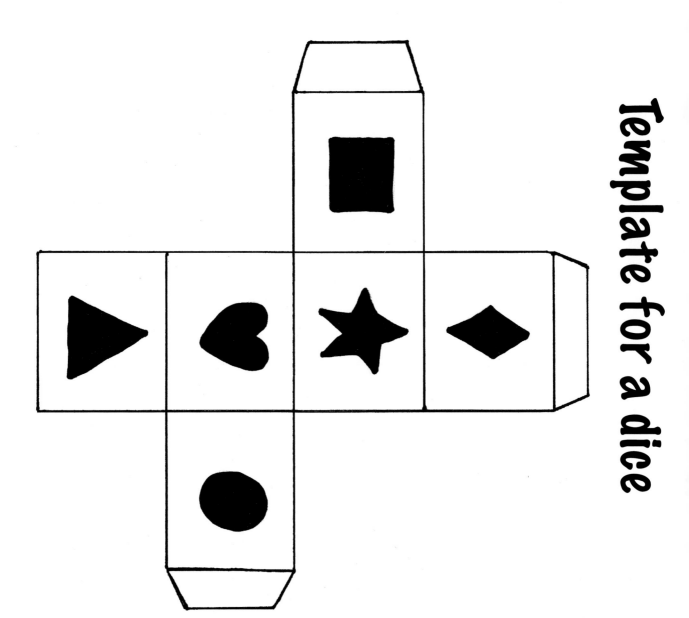

Template for a dice

Emotions cards

Say it in a sad voice	Say it in a happy voice	Say it in a tired voice
Say it in an angry voice	Say it in a quiet voice	Say it in a loud voice
Say it in a scared voice	Say it in an excited voice	Say it in a surprised voice
Say it in a bored voice	Say it in a high voice	Say it in a low voice

SECTION 2

SAYING S

Section 2: **Saying s**

Saying the speech sound s (1) (Listening and speaking activity)

Aim

To say the speech sound **s**.

How?

By giving the child opportunities to hear, and see, you say **s** and to copy you.

Resources

- Picture of nine seals and the sea (p42). Photocopy the page twice.

- Laminate one page and put small pieces of Velcro or Blu-Tack on each of the seals, and nine small pieces of Velcro or Blu-Tack on the sea. Cut out the line of seals from the other page and laminate it. Cut out the seals and put a small piece of Velcro or Blu-Tack on the back of each one. Stick each seal on top of a seal on the picture of the seals and the sea.

- Picture of nine Sams and nine surfboards (p43). Photocopy the page twice. Laminate one page and put small pieces of Velcro or Blu-Tack on each of the Sams, and nine small pieces of Velcro or Blu-Tack on the surfboard. Cut out the line of Sams from the other page and laminate it. Cut out the nine Sams and put a small piece of Velcro on the back of each one. Stick each Sam on top of a Sam on the picture of the nine Sams and nine surfboards.

- Picture of nine sausages and three saucepans (p44). Photocopy the page twice. Laminate one page and put small pieces of Velcro or Blu-Tack on each of the sausages, and three small pieces of Velcro or Blu-Tack on each saucepan. Cut out the line of sausages from the other page and laminate it. Cut out the sausages and put a small piece of Velcro or Blu-Tack on the back of each one. Stick each sausage on top of a sausage on the picture of nine sausages and three saucepans.

- Pictures of monsters' pawprints to photocopy, cut out and laminate (p45).

- Pictures of lily pads to photocopy, cut out and laminate (p46).

- Hand prints to photocopy (p47).

- Heads without hair to photocopy (p48).

- Aliens to photocopy (p49).

- Coloured pencils/pens.

Instructions

1. Read the instruction at the top of the page to the child. For example: *Put a seal in the sea and say* **s**. Before you carry out the instruction, say 'My turn!' so that the child knows you are going to do the task first. Then take a seal, stick it on the sea and say **s**.

2. When you have finished your go, say 'Your turn!' so that the child knows it is his go. The child takes a seal, puts it on the sea and says **s**. Take turns until all the seals are on the sea.

Variations

Listening activities

- Tell the child to listen carefully and put a seal on the sea when you say **s**. Count silently to at least four and then say **s**. When the child hears you say **s**, he takes a seal and puts it on the sea. If the child finds this activity hard, demonstrate it on a toy or puppet. For example, tell the toy or puppet to listen and put a seal on the sea when you say **s**. This gives the child an opportunity to watch the activity before he has a go. It also helps to reduce any feelings of anxiety he might have about taking part in the activity.

- To make this listening activity harder, ask the child to listen carefully and put a seal on the sea when you say **s** but this time say at least four other speech sounds before you say **s**. For example: **m d p k s**. Leave pauses between each speech sound to help the child listen for **s**.

- Try reversing the activity so that the child asks you, or the puppet or toy, to listen and put a seal on the sea when he says **s**.

- Photocopy the pictures of monsters' paw prints or lily pads. Laminate them, cut them out and put them on the floor. Carry out the listening activities described above. When the child hears you say **s**, he jumps on a paw print or lily pad.

- Photocopy one of the colouring pictures – the hands with lots of rings on the fingers, the aliens or the bald heads. When the child hears you say **s**, he colours in one of the rings (or draws an eye on an alien or draws a strand of hair on a bald head).

Saying the speech sound s (2) (Listening and speaking activity)

Aim

To say the speech sound **s**.

How?

By giving the child opportunities to hear, and see, you say **s** and to copy you.

Resources

- Template for a speech sound dice (50).

- Hand prints to photocopy (p47).

- Heads, without hair, to photocopy (p48).

- Aliens to photocopy (p49).

- Coloured pencils or pens.

- Pictures of monsters' paw prints (p45) to photocopy, cut out and laminate.

- Pictures of lily pads to photocopy, cut out and laminate (p46).

- Long and short pictures (pp51–53).

Instructions

1. Make a dice using the template. If the child cannot say any of the speech sounds on the template (**m, n, w, d, t, k**) use a blank template and write speech sounds that the child can say on it. For instance, you could put three speech sounds instead of six, eg **m, m, n, n, t, t**.

2. Choose a template to photocopy for the activity, eg colouring rings on fingers, drawing hair on a head.

3. Roll the dice to choose a speech sound, eg **m**.

4. Choose two colour pencils, eg orange and blue. Say the speech sound **s** and draw a strand of hair on one of the heads. Change colour pencils, say the speech sound that you rolled on the dice, eg **m**, and draw a second strand of hair on the head. Do this ten times so that you draw five orange hairs and say **s** five times, and draw five blue hairs and say **s** five times (**s, m, s, m, s, m, s, m, s, m**).

5. Take turns to say the two speech sounds and draw a hair on the head (or colour in a ring, or draw an eye on the alien).

Variations

- Use the activity as a listening game, eg 'When I say **s**, colour in a ring.'

- Use the activity to practise saying **s**. For example, take it in turns to say **s** and colour a ring.

- Say **s** and draw a strand of hair on a head. Change colours and say the speech sound you rolled on the dice, eg **m**, and draw another strand of hair. The child then says **s** and draws a strand of hair on the same head, changes colour and says the speech sound you rolled on the dice, eg **m**, and draws another strand of hair. Take it in turns until you have drawn at least twelve strands of hair on the head and said the speech sounds six times each.

- Take it in turns to say the two speech sounds, eg **s** and **m**, six times, drawing strands of hair on the head after you have said each one.

- When you and the child have both had a go, there should be twelve strands of hair on the head.

Tips

*Help! The child says **t** instead of **s**! What can you do?*

Children often say **t** instead of **s**. For example, they may say **tea** instead of **sea**. Developmentally, children say **t** before they say **s**. The speech sound **t** is a short speech sound whereas the speech sound **s** is a long speech sound. Help the child hear the difference between long and short sounds by playing listening games. For example:

- Photocopy a set of long and short pictures (pp51–53), eg long and short dog, or long and short hair, or long and short snake, and show the child. Think of at least two other examples of long and short: a giraffe has long legs and a sausage dog has short legs; you can wear a short skirt or a long skirt; a snake is long and a worm is short. Play a long sound on a shaker or bells. Then play a short sound. Repeat a few times and then say 'Listen to the shaker. If you hear a long sound, point to the long hair. If you hear a short sound, point to the short hair.' If the child points to the correct picture, he could colour in part of the picture.

- The child makes a long snake out of Plasticine or playdough. If he hears a long sound he puts a leg on the long snake and if he hears a short sound he puts a leg on the short snake.

- Draw a long snake and a short snake. The child colours in a stripe on the long snake if he hears a long sound. He colours in a stripe on the short snake if he hears a short sound.

- Use different instruments in listening games, eg a drum (short), a whistle (can be long or short depending on how you blow it), a tambourine (short if you use the top, long if it has bells on the sides).

When the child can consistently recognise short sounds (eg 70 per cent of the time or seven times out of 10), introduce speech sounds.

- Exaggerate **s** (**sssssssssss**) to help the child hear that it is a long sound. Carry out the same activities that you did with instruments but use a long and a short speech sound. Start with a short sound that is very different from **s**. This will help the child hear the different lengths of the speech sounds, eg **s** and **b**, **s** and **k**, **s** and **g**. Then carry out the activities with **s** (long speech sound) and **t** (short speech sound).

- Try giving the child more information about the speech sound **s**. For example: 'You said **t**. That's a short sound. Look at my mouth when I say **t**. Am I lifting the back of my tongue or the front? That's right, I am lifting the front of my tongue. I'm lifting it to touch just behind my top teeth. Look again. It's a short sound: **t**, **t**, **t**. I said **s**. That's a long sound. Look at my mouth when I say **s**. Can you see my tongue? No, it's behind my teeth. It's not touching my teeth. It's very close to the top of my mouth, but it is not touching the top of my mouth. Listen: **sssss**. Can you hear it is hissy? That's because the air is pushed out of this small space. Listen: **sssss**.' Use a mirror to help the child copy you.

*Help! The child makes a slushy sound when he says **s**. What can you do?*

- Discuss this with your local speech and language therapist.

My progress

Date	I can ...	☺/☹	I need to work on ...
	Listen carefully and put a seal in the sea when I hear **s** without any help.		
	Listen carefully and put a seal in the sea when I hear **s** with help.		
	Listen carefully to different speech sounds, eg **m d p k s**, and put a seal in the sea when I hear **s** without any help.		
	Listen carefully to different speech sounds, eg **m d p k s**, and put a seal in the sea when I hear **s** with help.		
	Say **s** without any help.		
	Say **s** with help.		
	Say **s** with other speech sounds, eg I can say s **m s m s m s m s m** without any help.		
	Say s with other speech sounds, eg I can say **s m s m s m s m s m** with help.		

What's the next step?

- I can listen carefully and put a seal in the sea when I hear **s** without any help. I can listen carefully to different speech sounds, eg **m d p k s**, and put a seal in the sea when I hear **s** without any help. **Move on to Section 3 and start listening activities.**

- I can listen carefully and put a seal in the sea when I hear **s** with help. I can listen carefully to different speech sounds, eg **m d p k s**, and put a seal in the sea when I hear **s** with help. **Carry on playing listening games from Section 2, but start to gradually include listening games from Section 3.**

- I can say **s** without any help. I can say **s** with other speech sounds, eg I can say **s, m, s, m, s, m, s, m, s, m** without any help. **Start Section 3: Saying s at the beginning of short words, eg sea, saw.**

- I can say **s** with help. I can say **s** with other speech sounds, eg I can say **s, m, s, m, s, m, s, m** with help. **Carry on working on activities in Section 2 to practise saying s and doing mouth exercises from Section 1.**

When the child can say s at least 70 per cent of the time, gradually introduce activities from Section 3.

Put a seal in the sea and say s

Put Sam on a surfboard and say s

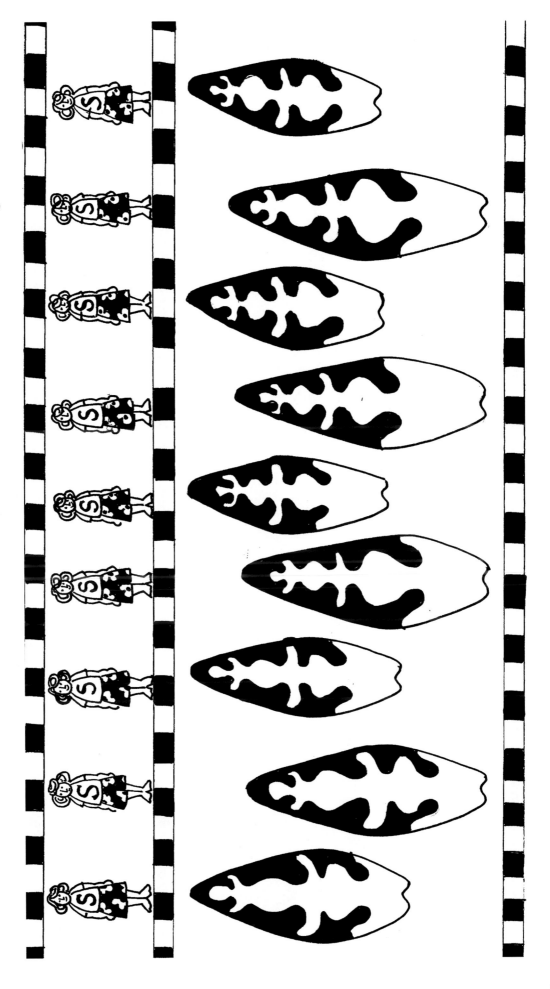

Put a sausage in a saucepan and say s

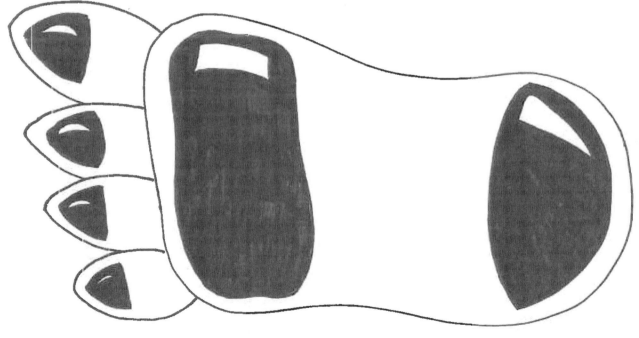

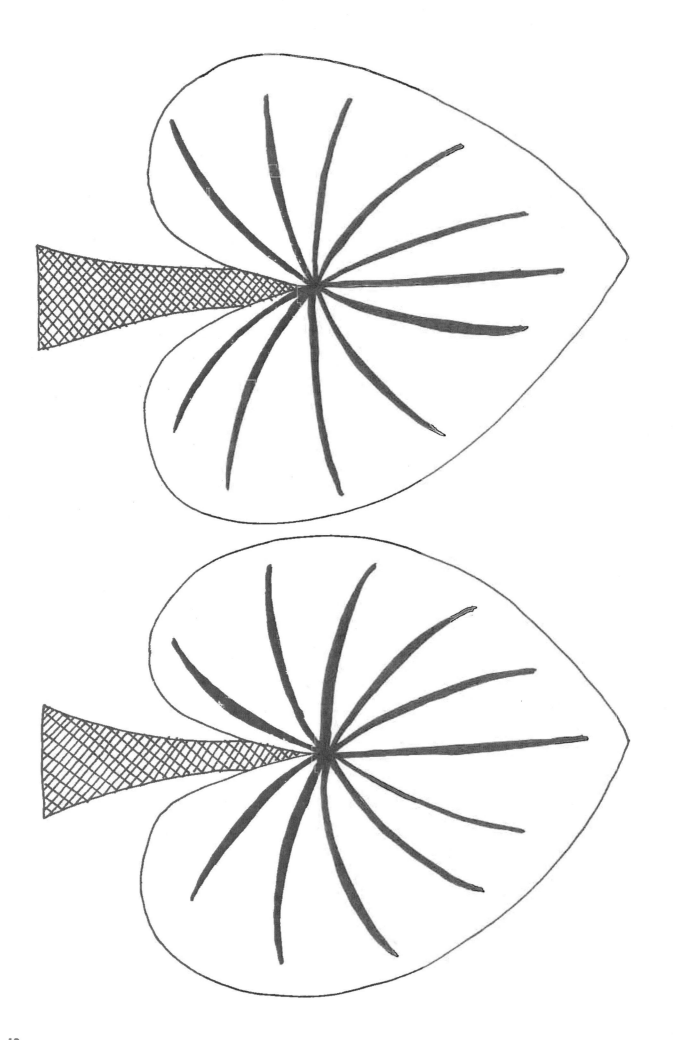

Say s and colour in a ring

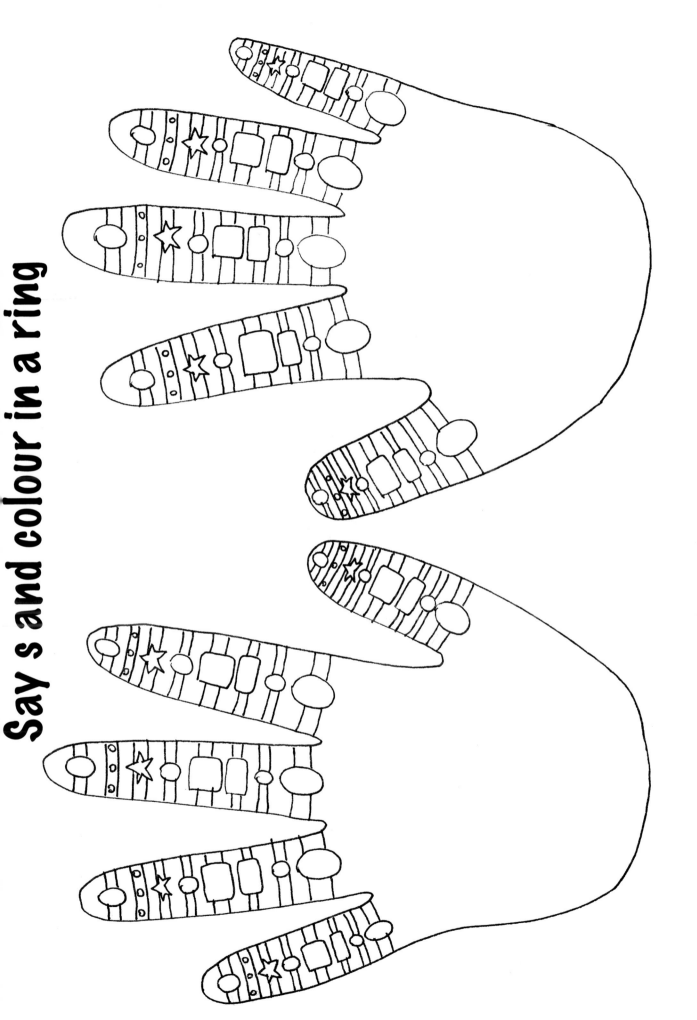

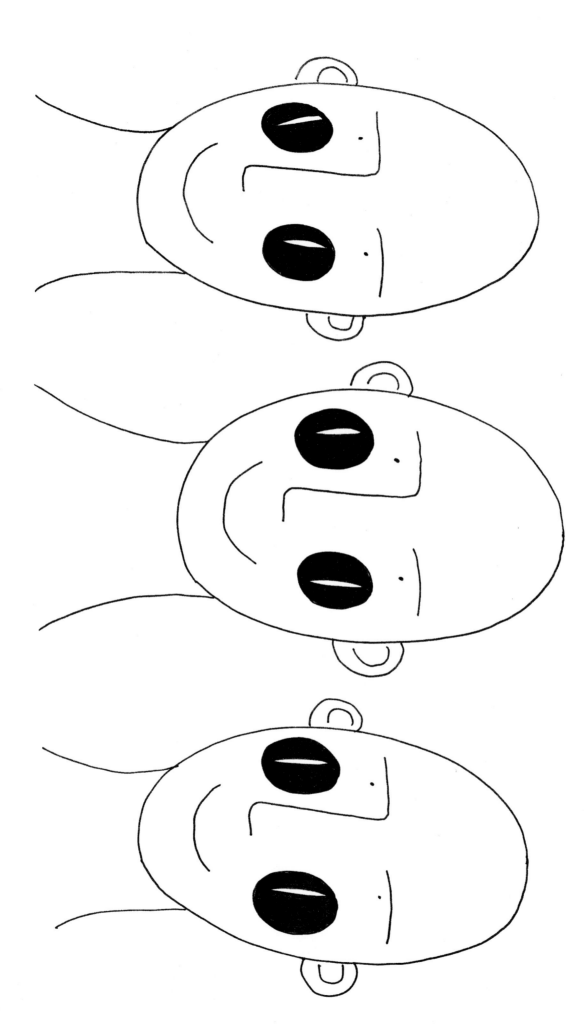

Say s and draw a strand of hair on a head

Say s and draw an eye on the alien

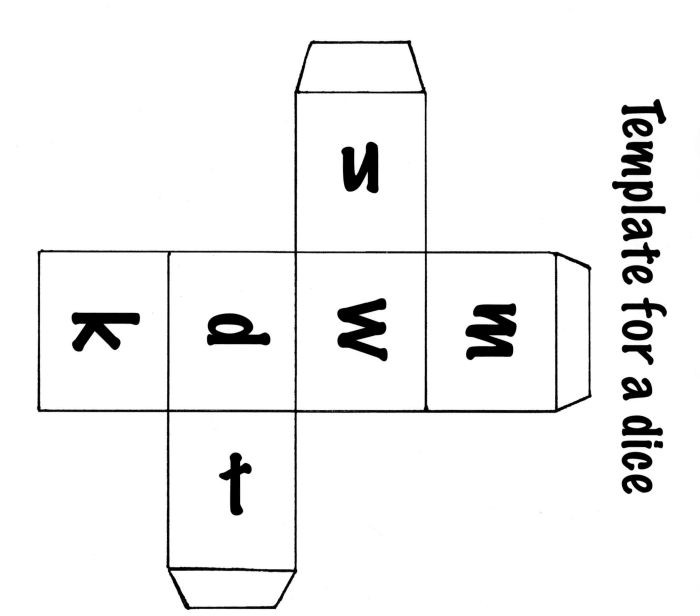

Template for a dice

Look!

short

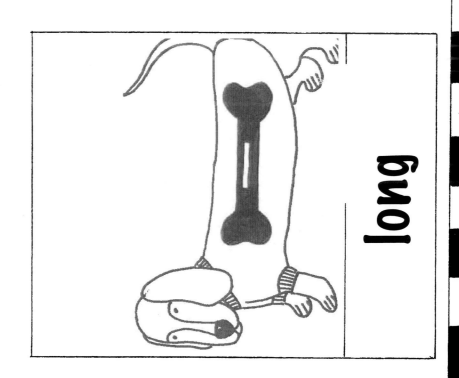

long

long

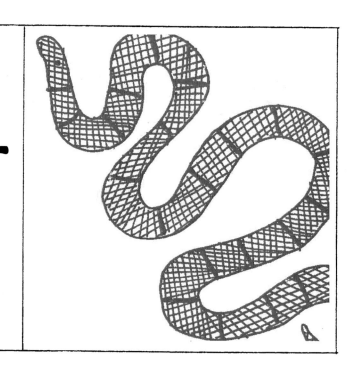

short

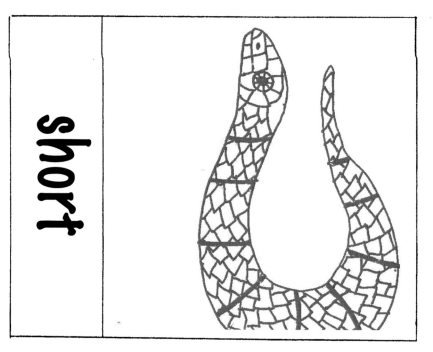

Look!

Look!

short

long

SAYING S AT THE BEGINNING OF SHORT WORDS

Section 3: Saying s at the beginning of short words

What's the picture? (Speaking activity)

Aim
To say short words that begin with the speech sound **s**: **saw**, **Si**, **sow**, **sew**, **Sue**, **soy**, **sea**, **say**.

How?
By giving the child opportunities to hear, and see, you say short words that begin with **s** and to practise saying the words.

Resources
- Large pictures of short words that begin with **s** (pp69–72).

- Small pictures of short words that begin with **s** (pp73–74).

- Page of two doors with question marks on each one and the instruction *What's the picture?* (p81). You will need to photocopy this page and laminate it, then cut along three sides of the doors so that you can open them to reveal a picture.

- The page of emotions (p31), eg *happy, sad, angry*. You will need to photocopy this page and cut it into cards.

Instructions
1. Put the page with the doors on top of a page of large pictures of words that begin with **s**, eg **saw** and **sew**.

2. Read the instruction at the top of the page to the child: *What's the picture? Open the door and see.* Before you open the door to see what the picture is, say 'My turn!' so that the child knows you are going first. Open the first door to reveal the picture and name it, eg 'Look! **Saw!**', so that the child has an opportunity to hear you say **s** at the beginning of a short word.

3. When you have finished your go, say to the child 'Your turn!' so that she knows that it is her go to open the door and name the picture behind it.

4. Put the picture of the doors over the next page of large pictures, eg **sea** and **say**, and take it in turns to open a door and name the picture behind it.

   Follow this procedure to name all the pictures for this activity.

Variations

- Put the laminated doors over two large pictures. Ask the child to guess what the picture is before she opens the door to see. For example: 'What do you think the picture is? I think it is the **sea**.'

- Tell the child to close her eyes and put a small picture of a word beginning with **s** behind each door. Then ask her to open her eyes and open the doors, but to guess what the picture is before she opens the door.

- Turn the emotion cards face down. Take it in turns to turn a card over, eg *say it in an angry voice*, and choose a large picture, eg **sea**. Say the word in the emotion on your card, eg say **sea** in an angry voice!

- Take it in turns to choose an emotion card. Do not show your card to anyone. Choose a picture, eg **Sue**. Say the word in the emotion on your card, eg say **Sue** in a sad voice. Your partner has to guess the emotion.

Tips

*Help! The child says **tea** instead of **sea**. What can you do?*

- Don't expect the child to be able to say **s** in words immediately. Give her plenty of opportunities to hear words that begin with **s**. You could try to use the words you are working on several times in conversation. For example: 'Look! The **sea**! Look at the big waves on the **sea**. I think the **sea** is really cold today! I like swimming in the **sea**, but I wouldn't swim in it today!'

- See advice in Section 2 for helping children to say **s**.

- If the child can say **s** most of the time, eg 70 per cent of the time, break the word into two parts, eg **s** + **ea**. Say the two parts leaving a pause between them: **s** (pause) – **ea**. Put two fingers on the table in a V shape, touch the first finger when you say **s** and touch the second finger when you say **ea**. Ask the child to copy you. Gradually make the pause shorter and bring your fingers closer together until your fingers are touching and there is no pause between **s** and **ea**: ie you are saying **sea**.

- If the child finds it very hard to blend and says **stea** or **sdea**, try saying **s** + **hea** instead of **s** + **ea**, ie insert the speech sound **h** in front of the vowels.

Help! The child won't try to say the words because she thinks she will make mistakes. What can you do?

- If the child gets anxious in activities and games, or is very unconfident, try using a puppet or a toy in sessions to reduce stress for her. Carry out the activities with the puppet or toy so that the child can watch and listen, but is not under any pressure to talk.

*Did you know that some children find it easier to say **s** at the end of words?*

- If the child is finding it very difficult to say **s** at the beginning of words, work on the words in Section 5 (words that end in **s**), eg **ace**, **ice**, before you work on words that begin with **s**.

Note: These tips can help you work on the words in this activity in Sections 4 and 5.

Hide Sam (Speaking and listening activity)

Aim
To provide more opportunities to hear and say **s** at the beginning of short words: **saw**, **Si**, **sow**, **sew**, **Sue**, **soy**, **sea**, **say**.

How?
By giving the child opportunities to hear, and see, you say short words that begin with **s** and to practise saying the words.

Resources
- Large pictures of short words that begin with **s** (pp69–72).

- Small pictures of short words that begin with **s** (pp73–74).

- Page of two doors with question marks on each one and the instruction *Close your eyes* (p82). You will need to copy this page, laminate it and cut along three sides of the doors so that you can open them to reveal a picture.

- A laminated picture of Sam (p74) with a small piece of Velcro or Blu-Tack on the back.

Instructions
1. Look at the pictures with the child: 'Look! **Sam**, **Sue** and **Si**.' Read the first part of the instruction at the top of the doors page: '*Close your eyes. I am going to hide **Sam**!*' Then stick the **Sam** on the picture of **Sue** or on the picture of **Si** and put the door over it. Read the rest of the instruction to the child: '*Open your eyes! Where's **Sam**?*' The child has to name the picture that she thinks **Sam** is on, eg '**Sue**' and then open the door to see if she is right or not. Play this game several times, varying the pictures that you use.

2. Reverse the game. Say to the child: 'Your turn. I'll close my eyes and you hide **Sam**!' Let the child have several turns at hiding **Sam**. To vary the pictures that you use in the game, put a small picture behind each door so that the child cannot predict what the pictures will be.

Tip

To make this a more challenging speaking game, offer a choice of pictures when the child is listening and guessing where Sam is, eg 'Where's **Sam**? **Sue** or **Si**?' When you reverse the game and the child is speaking and you are listening, she has to offer you a choice, eg 'Where's **Sam**? **Sea** or **say**?' Offering choices gives the child opportunities to say **s** at the beginning of more words.

Variations

If the child finds this activity hard, play it as a listening game. Ask her to close her eyes while you hide Sam on one of the pictures, eg **sow**. Ask the child to open her eyes and tell her where Sam is: 'Turn your listening ears on! Are you ready? **Sam** is on **sow**.' She then finds Sam. Use a toy or puppet to play this with younger children.

Tell the toy or puppet where Sam is and the child helps the toy or puppet find him.

Show the child at least two small pictures, eg **Sue** and **sea**. Name the pictures. Ask the child to close her eyes while you put a Sam under one of the pictures. Ask the child to open her eyes and ask her 'Where's **Sam**?' The child names the picture that she thinks Sam is under, eg '**sea**' and looks under the picture to see if she is right or not.

Show the child at least four small pictures. Name the pictures, eg '**Sea**. **Sue**. **Saw**. **Soy**.' Then tell the child you are going to hide two Sams. Ask her to close her eyes while you put a **Sam** under two of the pictures.

Ask the child to open her eyes and ask her 'Where are the **Sams**?' The child names the pictures that she thinks a Sam is under, eg '**saw** and **soy**' and looks to see if she is right or not. You can increase the number of pictures and the number of Sams in the game.

Remember to give the child a turn at hiding a Sam for you to find.

Tip

To give the child opportunities to say **s** at the beginning of more words, ask her 'Where are the **Sams**? Are they under **sea**, **Sue**, **saw** or **soy**?' This provides her with a model to copy when she is hiding the Sams and you are finding them.

What did I say? (Listening and speaking activity)

Aim
To say short words that begin with the speech sound **s**: **saw, Si, sow, sew, Sue, soy, sea, say**.

How?
By giving the child opportunities to hear, and see, you say short words that begin with **s** and to practise saying the words.

Resources
At least two sets of the small pictures of short words that begin with **s** (pp73–74).

Instructions
You are the speaker and the child is the listener in these activities.

1. Choose two pictures, eg **sea** and **sew**. Put them on the table in front of the child and name them for her: '**Sea. Sew**'. Tell the child to listen carefully and then you name one of the pictures placed in front of her, eg '**Sew**'.

   Then say 'What did I say?' The child listens and points to, or holds up, or puts a counter on the word she heard you say.

2. When you think the child is ready to listen and remember more words, choose three pictures, eg **sea, sew** and **Sue**. Put them on the table in front of the child and name them for her: '**Sea. Sew. Sue**'. Tell the child to listen carefully and then you name two of the pictures placed in front of her, eg '**Sue. Sea**'. Then say 'What did I say?' The child listens and points to, or holds up, or puts a counter on the words she heard you say. Increase the number of words to make the activity more challenging when you think the child is ready.

Variations
To make the activity more challenging, present at least three pictures to the child. Write down the words in the order you are going to say them, not in the order they appear in front of the child. For example, if the pictures in front of the child are **Sue, sea, sew**, you might write down **sea, sew, Sue**. Read out the words that you have written down: '**Sea. Sew. Sue**'. The child listens and arranges the pictures correspondingly, ie to match what you said (**sea, sew, Sue**).

Give the same pictures to yourself and to the child. You will need at least three, eg **Si, soy, say**. Place a barrier between yourself and the child so that you cannot see each other's pictures. Arrange your pictures without the child seeing. Name the pictures in the order you have arranged them, eg '**Soy. Say. Si**'. The child listens and arranges her pictures to match what you have said. Remove the barrier and see if the child's pictures are in the same order as yours! Vary the activity by, for example, giving the child four pictures but only saying three of them. Reverse the game so that the child is the speaker and you are the listener.

Tips

Help! The child can't remember what you said! What can you do?

- Start this activity by asking the child to remember one picture. Show her two pictures, eg **Sue** and **sea**, and name one of the pictures, eg **sea**. The child listens and points to the one that she heard. If she can do this easily, make the activity more challenging by presenting the child with three pictures, eg **Sue**, **sea**, **sow**, and naming two of them, eg '**Soy. Sue**'. Gradually increase the number of pictures so that the child has to remember more words.

Help! The child can't write the words! What can you do?

- To take part in this activity, children have to be able to read what they have written to you, but this does not mean that they have to spell the words correctly. For example, they might write **so** for **sew** or **soo** for **Sue**. Ask an adult or another child to help.

- Draw pictures of the words that you are going to say to the child, instead of writing the words. The child can draw pictures of the words she is going to say in the activity. She might need some help from an adult or another child.

Help! It is really hard work to get the child to do these activities! What can you do?

- Make sure you don't do these activities for too long. If the child finds it hard to concentrate, keep the activities short and fun!

- Offer a reward to the child if she does, say, one activity. Choose a reward that you know she will enjoy, eg blowing bubbles, playing with Lego for five minutes, colouring a picture, running round the playground. Gradually increase the number of activities she has to do in order to get the reward!

Note: These tips can help you work on the words in this activity in Sections 4, 5 and 6.

What's the word? (Listening activity)

Aim

To say short words that begin with the speech sound **s**: **saw**, **Si**, **sow**, **sew**, **Sue**, **soy**, **sea**, **say**.

How?

By giving the child opportunities to hear, and see, you say short words that begin with **s** and to practise saying the words.

Resources

At least two sets of the small pictures of short words that begin with **s** (pp73–74).

Instructions

This activity is for children aged four and a half upwards.

1. Lay a set of the small pictures in front of the child. Name them with the child so that she can hear you say the words before you start the activity.

2. Tell the child to listen carefully and point to the picture you are naming. Break words into the first speech sound, **s**, and the vowel, eg '**s – aw**'. Leave a short pause between **s** and the vowel to help the child carry out this task.

    The child has to put the **s** and the vowel together in her head to make the word, **saw**, and then point to the picture of a saw.

3. When the child is familiar with this activity, ask her to put the sounds together silently in her head, eg **s – aw**, point to the picture and say the word out loud: '**saw**'.

Variations

Give one set of the small pictures to yourself and one to the child.

Choose at least three pictures. Do not show the child the pictures you have chosen. Place a barrier between yourself and the child so that you cannot see each other's pictures. Arrange your pictures without the child seeing them on your side of the barrier, eg **sea**, **soy**, **Sue**. Tell the child to listen carefully, find the pictures you say and put them on her side of the barrier. Break each word into the first sound, **s**, and the vowel, eg '**s – ea, s – oy, S – ue (s – oo)**'. The child has to put the **s** and the vowel together in her head, find the picture and put it behind her barrier. When you have finished ask the child to say what the pictures are. Remove the barrier to see if they are the same as your pictures.

Tips

Help! The child keeps pointing to the wrong pictures! What can you do?

This activity might be very new for the child. Help her get used to it, and reduce any pressure she might be feeling, by using a toy or a puppet. Follow the instructions with the toy or puppet, so that the child can watch and listen. When the toy or puppet points to a picture, say 'Hold on a minute'. Turn to the child and say, for example: '**S – aw**. Let's put them together, **s** [pause] **aw, saw**! Did the puppet point to the **saw**? He did, didn't he? Clever puppet! He got it right!'

When the child is more familiar with the activity, the puppet or toy can start to make some mistakes. For example: you say '**s –ea**' and the puppet points to the picture of Sue. Check the puppet/toy's answer with the child and see if she can help the puppet by pointing to the right picture (sea).

*Help! When the child blends **s** and **aw**, she says **tore** or **door**! What can you do?*

This is primarily a listening activity, not a speaking activity. If the child points to the right picture, eg **saw**, then you know that she has blended **s** and **aw** together correctly in her head. The child said **tore** or **door** because she cannot say **s** in words yet. Say the word correctly for the child so that she has another opportunity to hear it and then ask her to repeat the word. For example: '**Saw**. [child repeats] Good work! **S – aw. Saw**! You got it!'

Roll and say (Speaking activity)

Aim
To say short words that begin with the speech sound **s**: **saw, Si, sow, sew, Sue, soy, sea, say**.

How?
By giving the child opportunities to hear, and see, you say short words that begin with **s** and to practise saying the words.

Resources
- A set of six small pictures (pp73–74) with shapes on the back, cut up and laminated (photocopy the sheet of shapes (p83) on to the back of the pictures so that they are double sided).

- A dice.

- Template for a dice with a different shape on each face (p30).

Instructions

1. Spread the pictures out in front of the child, face down so that you can see the shapes on the back.

2. Roll the dice with shapes on it. The shapes on the dice match the shapes on the back of the pictures. Turn over the picture that has the same shape as the dice, eg circle, so that you can see what the picture is, eg **sew**.

3. Roll the dice with numbers on it. You have to say the word on your picture, eg **sew**, the number of times that you throw on the dice, eg 5: '**sew, sew, sew, sew, sew**'. Make sure you have the first turn so that you can demonstrate the activity to the child.

Variations

Make the game competitive: the winner is the first person to say the names of all of the six pictures in the activity, ie to throw all of the shapes on the dice.

Roll the dice with shapes on it and turn over the picture that has the same shape on it, eg heart. Take it in turns to see how many times you can say the word in a minute. Use a one-minute salt timer.

A or B? (Listening activity)

Aim

To help the child hear the difference between the speech sound she wants to say in words, **s**, and the speech sounds she is saying in words, eg **t** or **d**. For example, she may want to say **sea**, but she says **tea**.

How?

By giving the child opportunities to hear, and see, you say short words that begin with **s** and short words that rhyme and start with **t** or **d** (depending on whether the child replaces **s** with **t** or with **d** in words).

Resources

- Pictures of words that start with **s**: **Sue, sea, saw, soy, sew, Si** (pp73–74).

- Pictures of words that start with **t** and rhyme with the words that start with **s**: **two, tea, tore, toy, toe, tie** (p75–77).

- Pictures of words that start with **d** and rhyme with the words that start with **s**: **do, die, door, day, dough, dee** (p78–80).

- Pictures of lily pads or monsters' footprints (pp45–46).

- Playdough or Plasticine.

- Stickers.

Instructions

1. Choose a pair of words. For example: if the child says **t** instead of **s** in words, choose pairs of rhyming words that begin with **s** and begin with **t** (**Sue** and **two**, **Si** and **tie**, **sea** and **tea**, **saw** and **tore**, **soy** and **toy**, **sew** and **toe**.)

   Photocopy the pictures and put them in front of the child.

2. Tell the child to listen carefully. Say the two words for her, eg 'Si. Tie'.

3. Give the child a sticker and ask her to listen again. Say one of the words, eg 'Si', and ask the child to put the sticker on the word she heard.

Tips

- If the child finds it very difficult to hear the difference between **s** and **t** at the beginning of words, try giving her more information about the two sounds and elongating **s** when you say it. For example: 'Listen. **Si**. That starts with a long sound. Listen again: **SSSSSSi**. I'm going to say a really long **s**. Ready? **SSSSSSSSSSSSSi**! **Tie**. That's not a long sound, is it? **Tie**. That's a short sound. I'm going to say them again Listen: **SSSSSSSSSi. Tie.**'

- If you work in a nursery or school and use visual support to help children learn phonics, for example the hand movements in Jolly Phonics to help children learn letters and sounds, use these with the child to help her distinguish between **s** and **t**. Keep trying this activity without the hand movements to see if the child can hear the difference without visual support.

- Ask your speech and language therapist to show you cued articulation for **s**, **t** and **d** and use it to give the child visual support in these listening activities.

Variations

- Put the pair of pictures you are working with on lily pads or monsters' footprints on the floor. The child listens and jumps on the one she heard.

- Put the pictures on the table or on the wall. The child points to the one she heard. With younger children, put a sticker or a ring on the finger they are going to point with and tell them that is their magic finger.

- Make two playdough or Plasticine snakes. Put a snake by each picture, eg **toe** and **sew**. The child listens and points to the one she heard. If she is right, she puts a playdough or Plasticine leg on the snake that is by the picture.

Help! The child points to the wrong picture? What can you do?

- Say the two words for her again, exaggerating the **s** at the beginning and using visual support such as the hand movements for Jolly Phonics or cued articulation to help her. Then say 'Listen again. **Tie**. Is that a long sound or a short sound? **Tie**. It's short. It's this one.' (Point to the picture of a tie.) Let her put a leg on the snake near the picture of a tie.

Tip
- Play listening games with the rhyming pairs of words from the list of games in Section 9, eg Catch a picture, Bowling, Goal!, Listen and colour.

My progress

Date	I can ...	☺/☹	I need to work on ...
	Listen carefully and hear short words that begin with **s**, eg **sea**, **say**, **soy**, without any help.		
	Listen carefully and hear short words that begin with **s**, eg **sea**, **say**, **soy**, with help.		
	Say **s** at the beginning of short words, eg **sea**, **say**, **soy**, without any help.		
	Say **s** at the beginning of short words, eg **sea**, **say**, **soy**, with some help.		

What's the next step?

- I can listen carefully and hear short words that begin with **s**, eg **sea**, **say**, **soy**, without any help. **Start Section 4.**

- I can listen carefully and hear short words that begin with **s**, eg **sea**, **say**, **soy**, with help. **Continue playing listening games from Section 3. Play listening games from the list of games in Section 9. When the child is able to listen and hear short words that begin with s without help at least 70 per cent of the time, gradually introduce listening activities from Section 4.**

- I can say **s** at the beginning of short words, eg **sea**, **say**, **soy**, without any help. **Start Section 4. Play speaking games from the list of games in Section 9, eg Pairs, Kim's game, Find the coin.**

- I can say **s** at the beginning of short words, eg **sea**, **say**, **soy**, with some help. **Continue playing talking games from Section 3 and carry on doing mouth exercises from Section 1. Play games from the list of games in Section 9. When the child is able to say s at the beginning of short words that begin with s without help at least 70 per cent of the time, gradually introduce speaking games from Section 4.**

Tip

- To check if the child can hear and/or say **s** at the beginning of short words 70 per cent of the time, see if she can hear or say words seven out of ten times. If you have fewer than ten words, see if the child can hear or say words, for example, four out of six times, or six out of eight times.

Look!

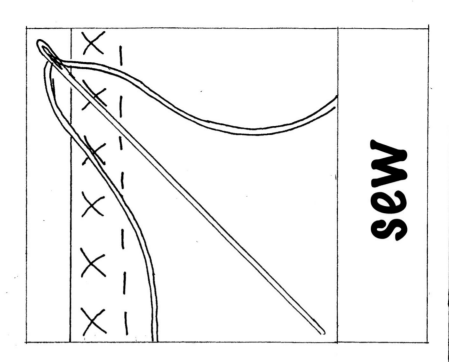

sew

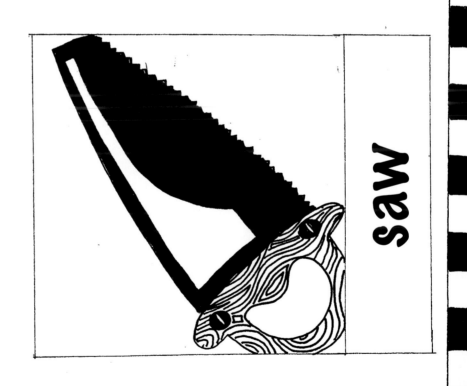

saw

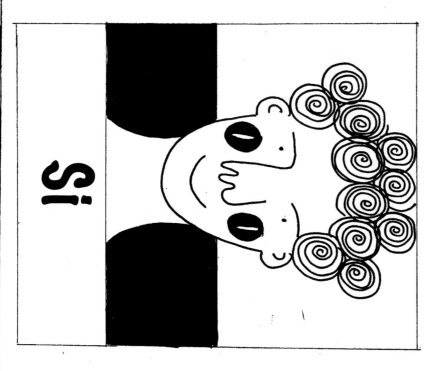

Si

Sue

Look!

70

Look!

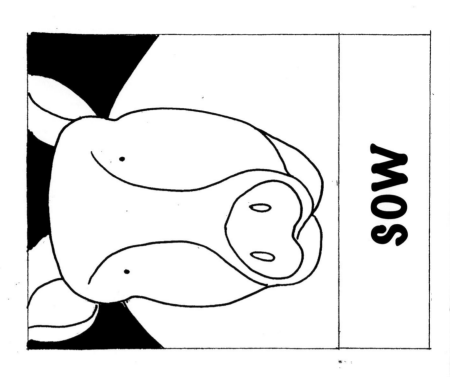

SOW

SOY

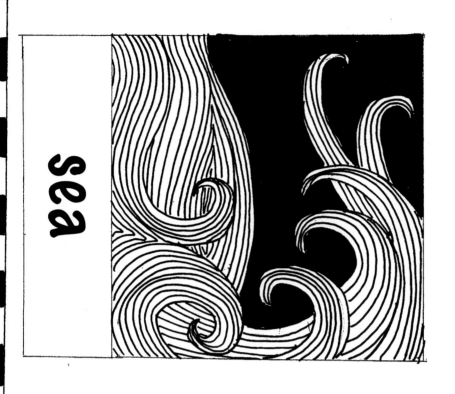

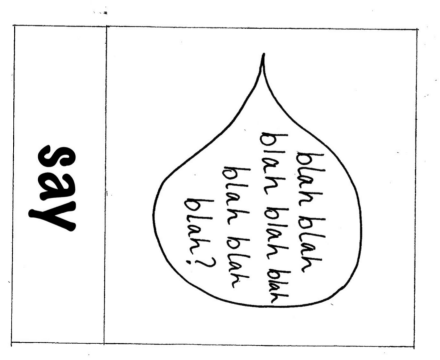

Look!

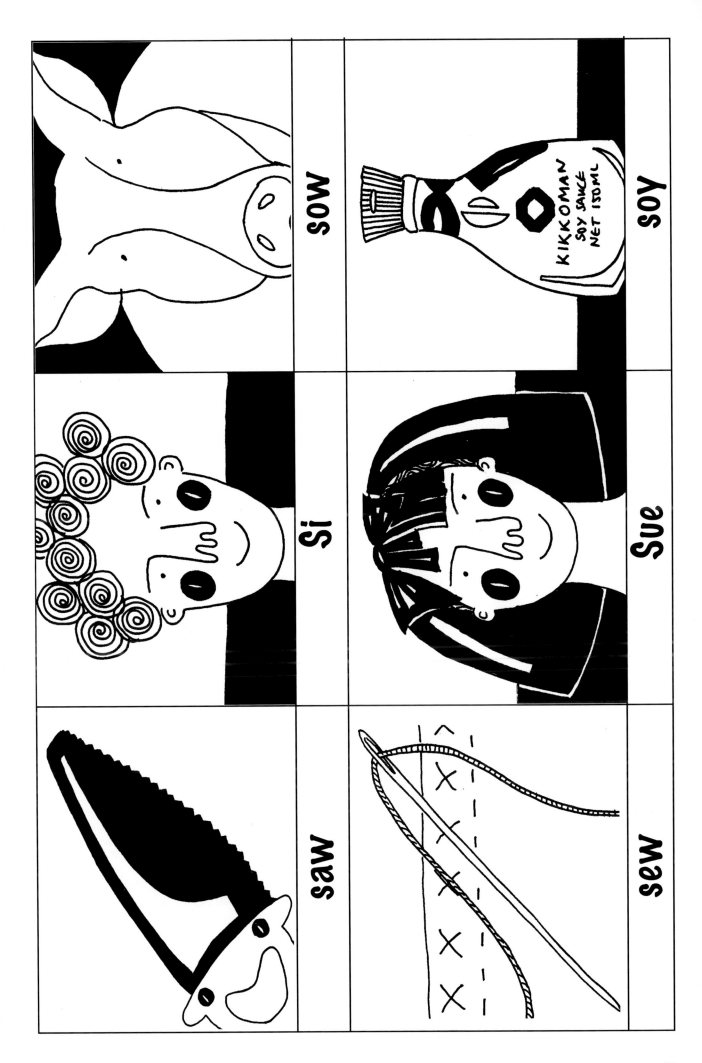

sow

SOY

Si

Sue

saw

sew

	sea	
	say	
	Sam	

Look!

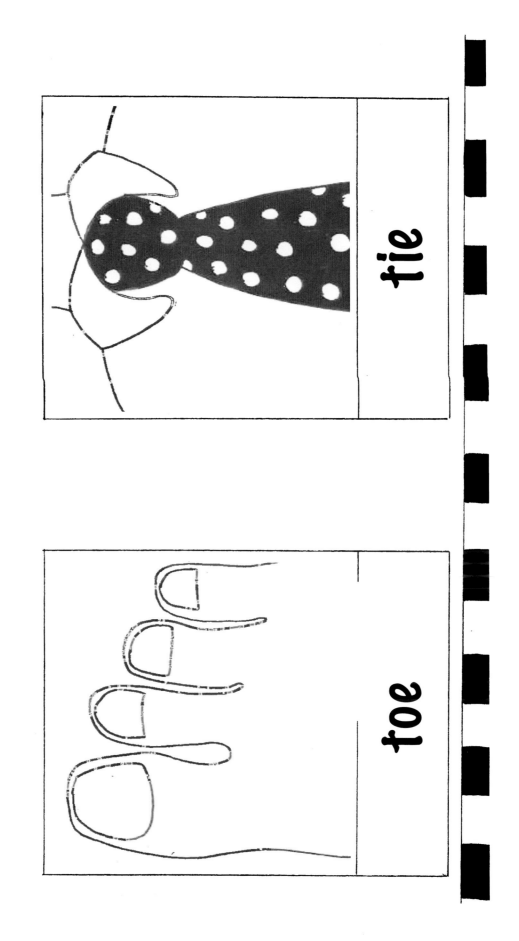

tie

toe

two

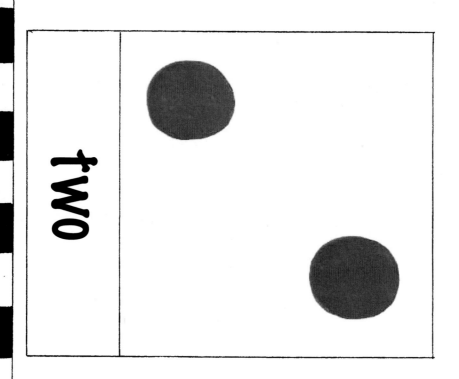

tea

Look!

Look!

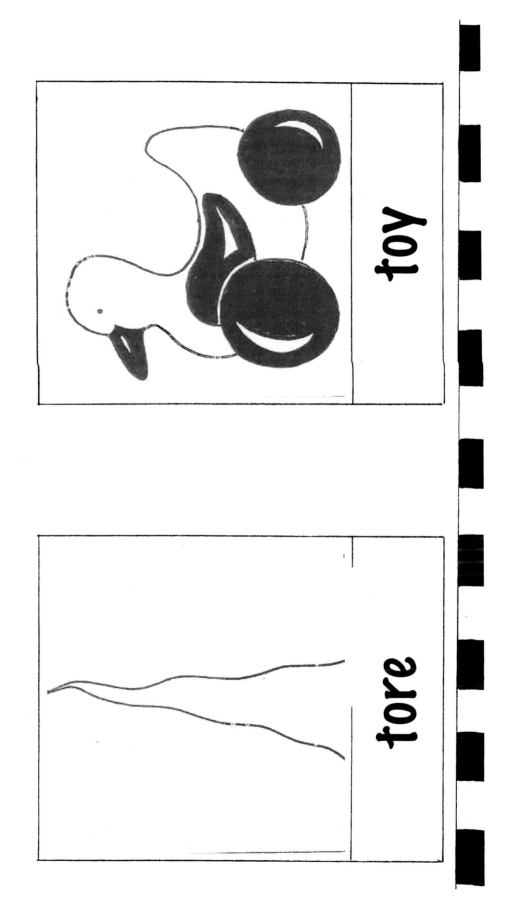

tore

toy

dough

dee

Look!

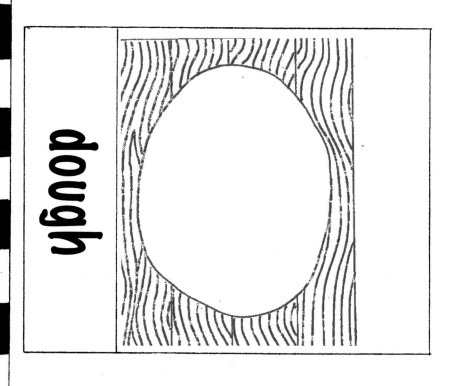

Look!

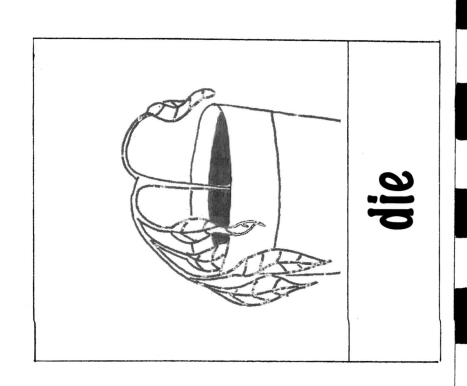

die

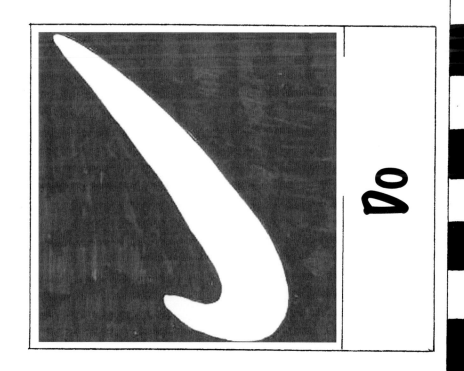

Do

door

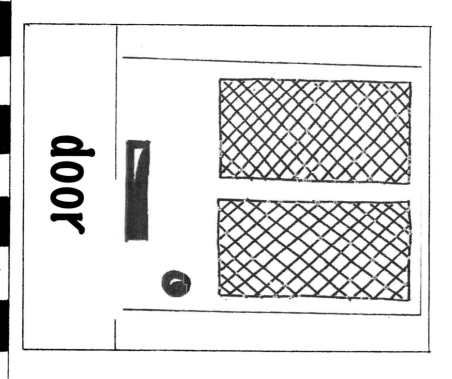

day

Look!

What's the picture? Open the door and see!

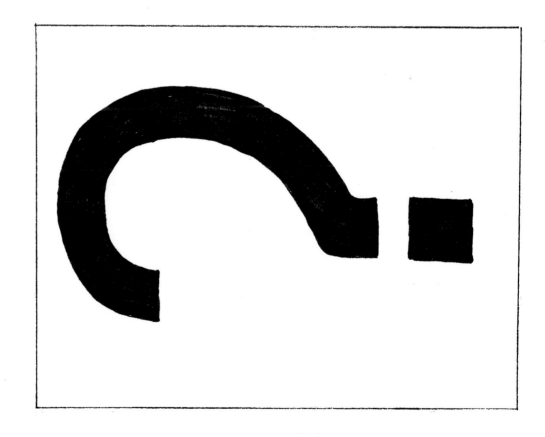

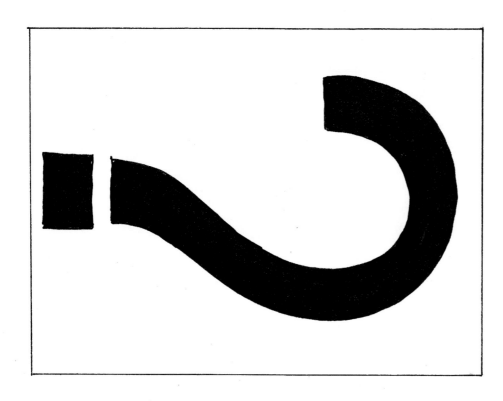

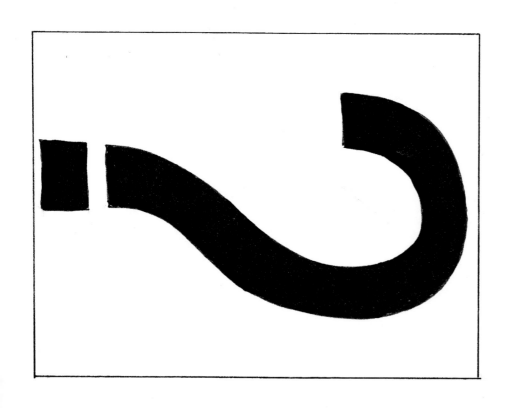

Close your eyes! I'm going to hide Sam!
Open your eyes! Where's Sam?

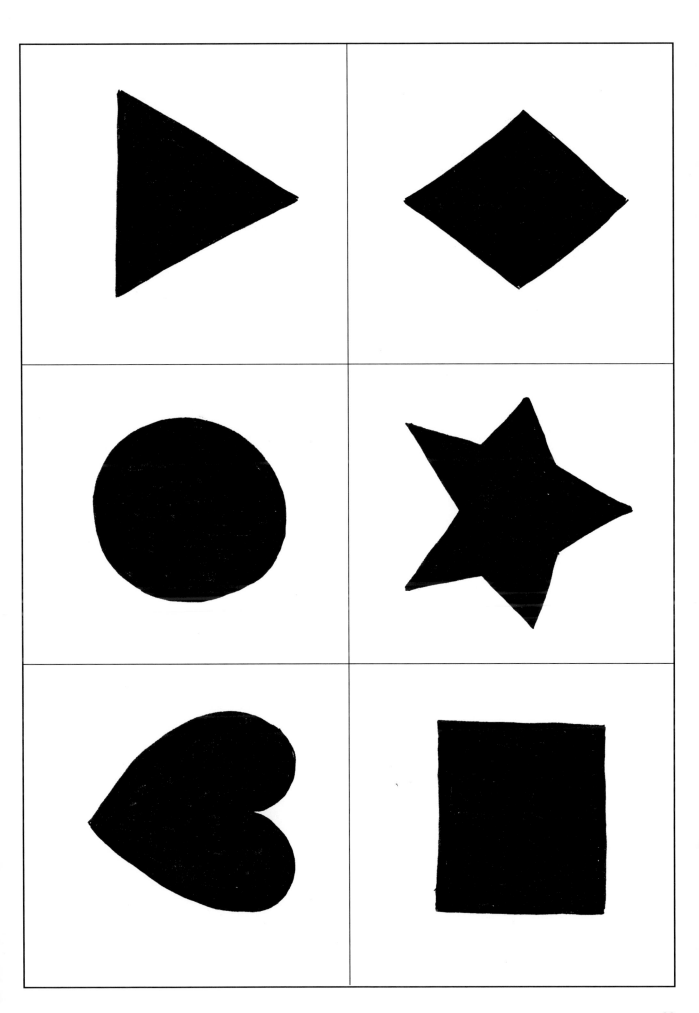

Jingles

Many children, especially young children, eg under five, benefit from listening to words that contain the speech sound they are learning to use, in this case **s**. Listening can help raise their awareness of the speech sound in words and so help them to say the speech sound.

At the end of Sections 3, 4, 5 and 6 of this book are some jingles that contain the words you have been working on with the child, for example in this section words that begin with **s**: **sea**, **saw**, **Sue**, **Si**, **sew**, **sow**, **soy**, **say**.

Ideas for using the jingles

Step 1: Choose one or two jingles that contain the words you have been working on with the child.

Step 2: Read the jingle to the child and look at the pictures together. Use gestures or signing to make the jingles more memorable for the child. Read at least one jingle at the same time in each session, perhaps at the end. Some children may benefit from hearing the same jingle every day for a week, whereas others may benefit from hearing one jingle for half the week and then hearing a new one for the rest of the week.

Tip
- Use your voice to make the jingles more interesting. For example: vary your pitch – say some words in a low voice, others in a high voice; vary your volume – say some words in a loud voice, others in a quiet voice. At this stage, there is no pressure on the child to talk. She can enjoy listening to the jingles without worrying about talking.

Step 3: When the child is making progress with the speech sound you are working on (for example, she is saying **s** at the beginning of short words 70 per cent of the time even if she needs some help), omit a word that contains **s** in a line of the jingle and leave a pause to see if the child can say the missing word. For example: 'Sue has a pet _____ (sow)'. Gradually increase the number of lines in which you are leaving a word out and waiting for the child to say it. For example: 'Sue has a pet _____ (sow). Sue's pet sow likes _____ (soy) _____ sauce'.

Tip
- If the child cannot remember the word, sound it out for her, eg '**s – oy**'. See if she can put the sounds together and say the word: '**soy**'.

Step 4: When the child can say the word you leave out most of the time, try omitting more than one word in lines to see if she can complete the jingles. For example: 'Sam the _____ (seal) likes to _____ (sing)'.

Tip

- Encourage the child to copy your gestures or signs as she says the jingles with you.

Step 5: When the child is able to say more than one word to complete sentences (step 4), see if she can remember an entire line of a jingle! Start with short lines! For example: Sue saw Si_____ (Si saw Sue).

Try taking it in turns to say a line each of short jingles!

Step 6: Try reading jingles with older children, eg six to seven years old.

Jingles with short words that begin with s

Jingle 1   (pictures on p70)

Listen

Sue saw Si

Si saw Sue

Sue, say hi to Si

Si, say hi to Sue

'Hi, Si' said Sue

'Hi, Sue' said Si

Bye, Sue

Bye, Si

Say the word

Sue saw _____ (Si)

Si saw _____ (Sue)

Sue, say hi to _____ (Si)

Si, say hi to _____ (Sue)

'Hi, Si' said _____ (Sue)

'Hi, Sue' said _____ (Si)

Bye, _____ (Sue)

Bye, _____ (Si)

Jingle 2 (pictures on p74)

Listen

Can you say see-saw see-saw see-saw?

Yes, I can.

Can you say see-saw Si see-saw Si see-saw Si?

Yes, I can

Can you say see-saw Si say see-saw Si say see-saw Si say?

Yes, I can

Can you say saw Si say see backwards?

No, I can't. Can you?

Say the word

Can you say see-saw see-saw see _____ (saw)?

Yes, I can

Can you say see-saw Si see-saw Si see-saw _____ (Si)?

Yes, I can

Can you say see-saw Si say see-saw Si say see-saw Si _____ (say)?

Yes, I can

Can you say saw Si say _____ (see) backwards?

No, I can't. Can you?

Jingle 3 (pictures on p71)

Listen

My friend Sue has a pet sow

Sue's pet sow likes soy sauce

Sue puts soy sauce on her sow's cereal

Sue puts soy sauce on her sow's sandwich

Sue puts soy sauce on her sow's pizza

Yuk! I don't want to eat at Sue's house, do you?

Say the word

My friend Sue has a pet _____ (sow)

Sue's pet sow likes _____ (soy) sauce

_____ (Sue) puts soy sauce on her sow's cereal

Sue puts _____ (soy) sauce on her sow's sandwich

_____ (Sue) puts soy sauce on her sow's pizza

Yuk! I don't want to eat at Sue's house, do you?

Jingle 4 (pictures on p73)

Listen

I say, I say, I say. Have you ever seen a sow that could sew?

No, I haven't

I say, I say, I say. Have you ever seen a sow swimming in the sea?

No, I haven't

I say, I say, I say. Have you ever seen a sow eating soy sauce?

Yes, I have

Really?

No!

Say the word

I say, I say, I say. Have you ever seen a sow that could _____ (sew)?

No, I haven't

I say, I say, I say. Have you ever seen a sow swimming in the _____ (sea)?

No, I haven't

I say, I say, I say. Have you ever seen a sow eating _____ (soy) sauce?

Yes, I have

Really?

No!

SECTION 4

SAYING S AT THE BEGINNING OF LONGER WORDS

Section 4: Saying s at the beginning of longer words

What's the picture? (Speaking activity)

Aim
To say longer words that begin with the speech sound **s: safe, seed, seal, sing, save, sack, sun, seat, Sam, soap, soup, Sid, sword, sock, sail, suit, sum, sad, sell, sip**.

How?
By giving the child opportunities to hear, and see, you say longer words that begin with **s** and to practise saying the words.

Resources
- Large pictures of longer words that begin with **s** (pp101–110).

- Small pictures of longer words that begin with **s** (pp117–120).

- Page of two doors with question marks on each one and the instruction *What's the picture?* (p81). You will need to photocopy this page and laminate it, then cut along three sides of the doors so that you can open them to reveal a picture.

- The page of emotions (p31), eg *happy, sad, angry*. You will need to photocopy this page and cut it into cards.

Instructions
1. Put the page with the doors on top of a page of large pictures of words that begin with **s**, eg **soap** and **soup**.

2. Read the instruction at the top of the page to the child: '*What's the picture? Open the door and see.*' Before you open the door to see what the picture is, say 'My turn!' so that the child knows you are going first. Open the first door to reveal the picture and name it, eg 'Look! **Soup**!', so that the child has an opportunity to hear you say **s** at the beginning of the word.

3. When you have finished your go, say to the child 'Your turn!' so that he knows that it is his go to open the door and name the picture behind it.

4. Put the picture of the doors over the next page of large pictures, eg **seed** and **safe**, and take it in turns to open a door and name the picture behind it. Follow this procedure to name all the pictures on the pages for this activity.

Variations

Put the laminated doors over two large pictures. Ask the child to guess what the picture is before he opens the door to see. For example: 'What do you think the picture is? I think it is the **sack**.'

Tell the child to close his eyes and put a small picture behind each door. Then ask him to open his eyes and open the doors, but to guess what the picture is before he opens the door.

Note: See advice in Section 3 for helping children to say **s** in words.

Roll and say (Speaking activity)

Aim

To say longer words that begin with the speech sound **s**: **safe, seed, seal, sing, save, sack, sun, seat, soap, soup, Sam, Sid, sword, sock, sail, suit, sum, sad, sell, sip**.

How?

By giving the child opportunities to hear, and see, you say longer words that begin with **s** and to practise saying the words.

Resources

- A set of six small pictures (pp117–120) with shapes on the back, cut up and laminated (photocopy the sheet of shapes (p83) on to the back of the pictures so that they are double sided).

- A dice.

- Template for a dice with a different shape on each face (p30).

Instructions

1. Spread the pictures out in front of the child, face down so that you can see the shapes on the back.

2. Roll the dice with shapes on it. The shapes on the dice match the shapes on the back of the pictures. Turn over the picture that has the same shape as the dice, eg circle, so that you can see what the picture is, eg **soap**.

3. Roll the dice with numbers on it. You have to say the word on your picture, eg **soap**, the number of times that you throw on the dice, eg 5. Make sure you have the first turn so that you can demonstrate the activity to the child.

Variations

- Make the game competitive: the winner is the first person to say the names of all of the six pictures in the activity, ie to throw all of the shapes on the dice.

- Roll the dice with shapes on it and turn over the picture that has the same shape on it, eg heart. Take it in turns to see how many times you can say the word in a minute. Use a one-minute salt timer.

Remember and say (Speaking and listening game)

Aim

To say longer words that begin with the speech sound **s**: **safe**, **seed**, **seal**, **sing**, **save**, **sack**, **sun**, **seat**, **soap**, **soup**, **Sam**, **Sid**, **sword**, **sock**, **sail**, **suit**, **sum**, **sad**, **sell**, **sip**.

How

By giving the child opportunities to hear, and see, you say words that begin with **s** and to practise saying the words.

Resources

- At least one set of the small pictures of words that begin with **s** (pp117–120).

Instructions

1. Look at the pictures of the longer words that begin with **s** and name them with the child.

2. Present at least two of the pictures to the child and name them, eg '**Sing. Sock**'. Tell the child to 'take a photo' of the pictures in his mind, ie use a mental camera, to help him remember them. Give him at least 30 seconds to look at the pictures. Then turn them over and ask the child if he can remember what they are. The child then names the pictures. Turn them over to see if he is right. Make this activity more challenging by increasing the number of pictures that the child has to remember.

Variations

- Give the same pictures to yourself and to the child. You will need at least four, eg **seed**, **safe**, **sun**, **sad**. Place a barrier between yourself and the child so that you cannot see each other's pictures. Arrange at least two of your pictures behind the barrier so that the child cannot see what they are. Name the pictures, eg '**Sun. Sad**'. Pause for a few seconds and then say: 'Ready, steady, go!' The child listens, then looks at his pictures, finds the ones he heard you name and lays them out on his side of the barrier. When you remove the barrier you will see if the child's pictures are the same as yours! Reverse the game so that the child names pictures for you to remember and arrange behind the barrier.

- Play Kim's game with the pictures (see instructions in Section 9, p262).

- Play Pairs (see instructions in Section 9, p262).

Note: These variations can be used with this activity in Section 5.

Listen and guess (Listening and speaking activity)

Aim
To say longer words that begin with the speech sound **s: safe**, **seed**, **seal**, **sing**, **save**, **sack**, **sun**, **seat**, **soap**, **soup**, **Sam**, **Sid**, **sword**, **sock**, **sail**, **suit**, **sum**, **sad**, **sell**, **sip**.

How?
By giving the child opportunities to hear, and see, you say words that begin with **s** and to practise saying the words.

Resources
- Two sets of small pictures of longer words that begin with **s** (pp117–120).

Instructions
1. Choose a picture, eg **sock**. Do not show it to the child. Place it face down in front of him.

2. Tell the child at least three things about the picture, eg 'You wear it. You wear it on your foot. It can be smelly!'

3. The child guesses what the picture is and turns it over to see if he is right. Reverse the game so that the child chooses a picture and describes it and you guess what it is.

Variations
- To make this activity less challenging for the child, put at least three pictures in front of him, eg **sock**, **sack**, **sum**. Choose one of the pictures to describe, eg **sum**. Do not tell the child which picture you have chosen. Tell him three things about the picture, eg 'You do this at school. You do this with numbers. You can add numbers together or take numbers away.' The child listens and points to the picture that he thinks you are describing, eg **sum**.

- To make this activity more challenging, choose at least three pictures.

- Do not show them to the child. Place them face down in front of him.

- Tell the child at least three things about the first picture. The child guesses what it is and turns it over to see if he is correct. Then tell them three things about the second picture. The child guesses and checks if he is right or not. Follow the same procedure for the third picture. Reverse the game, so that the child chooses at least three pictures and describes them to you.

- Place a barrier between you and the child. Make sure that you each have a set of the small pictures. Choose at least three pictures from your set, eg **sum**, **sun**, **seal**. Describe the pictures to the child, leaving a pause between each description so that he can find the one he thinks you are talking about in his set. When the child has found the picture he thinks you are describing, he puts it face up behind the barrier so that you cannot see it. When you have described all three pictures and the child has put three corresponding pictures behind the barrier, ask him to say what his pictures are, eg '**sum**, **sun**, **seal**'. Then remove the barrier to see if he has the same pictures as you. Reverse the game, so that the child chooses and describes three pictures and you listen.

What did I say? (Listening and speaking activity)

Aim
To say longer words that begin with the speech sound **s**: **safe**, **seed**, **seal**, **sing**, **save**, **sack**, **sun**, **seat**, **soap**, **soup**, **Sam**, **Sid**, **sword**, **sock**, **sail**, **suit**, **sum**, **sad**, **sell**, **sip**.

How?
By giving the child opportunities to hear, and see, you say longer words that begin with **s** and to practise saying the words.

Resources
- At least two sets of the small pictures of longer words that begin with **s** (pp117–120).

Instructions
1. Choose two pictures, eg **soup** and **safe**. Put them on the table in front of the child and name them for him: '**Soup. Safe**'. Tell the child to listen carefully and then you name one of the pictures placed in front of him, eg '**Soup**'. Then say 'What did I say?' The child listens and points to, or holds up, or puts a counter on the picture of the word he heard you say.

2. When you think the child is ready to listen and remember more words, choose three pictures, eg **soup**, **safe** and **sword**. Put them on the table in front of the child and name them for him: '**Soup. Safe. Sword**'. Tell the child to listen carefully and then you

name two of the pictures placed in front of him, eg '**Soup. Sword**'. Then say 'What did I say?' The child listens and points to, or holds up, or puts a counter on the words he heard you say.

Increase the number of words to make the activity more challenging when you think the child is ready.

Note: See Section 3 for variations and tips for this activity.

What's the word? (Listening activity)

Aim

To say longer words that begin with the speech sound **s**: **safe**, **seed**, **seal**, **sing**, **save**, **sack**, **sun**, **seat**, **soap**, **soup**, **Sam**, **Sid**, **sword**, **sock**, **sail**, **suit**, **sum**, **sad**, **sell**, **sip**.

How?

By giving the child opportunities to hear, and see, you say longer words that begin with **s** and to practise saying the words.

Resources

- At least two sets of the small pictures (pp117–120).

Instructions

This activity is for children aged four and a half upwards.

1. Lay a set of the small pictures in front of the child. Name them with the child, so that he can hear the words before you start the activity.

Tips

- Use at least three small pictures with younger children. Be flexible with the number of pictures you present at the beginning of the activity depending on the level of the child.

- The aim of this activity is to help the child say **s** at the beginning of longer words. Some children may have other speech sound difficulties. For example, they may say the speech sound **b** instead of **v** (**sabe** instead of **safe**), or they may say the speech sound **p** instead of **f** (**sape** instead of **safe**). However, you are working on saying **s** in words, so this is the only speech sound you need to focus on in these activities.

2. Tell the child to listen carefully and point to the picture you are naming. Break words into the first speech sound, **s**, and the rest of the word, eg '**s – uit**'. Leave a short pause between the speech sounds to help the child carry out this task. The child has to put the speech sounds together in his head to make the word, eg **suit**, and then point to the picture of a suit.

3. When the child is familiar with this activity, ask him to put the sounds together silently in his head, point to the picture and say the word out loud, eg '**suit**'.

Variations

- Give one set of the small pictures to yourself and one to the child. Choose at least three pictures. Do not show the child the pictures you have chosen. Place a barrier between yourself and the child so that you cannot see each other's pictures. Arrange your pictures without the child seeing them on your side of the barrier, eg **suit**, **seat**, **safe**. Tell the child to listen carefully, find the pictures you say and put them on his side of the barrier. Break each word into the first sound, **s**, and the rest of the word, eg '**s – uit**, **s – eat**, **s – afe**'. The child has to put the speech sounds together in his head, find the picture and put it behind his barrier. When you have finished, ask the child to say what the pictures are. Remove the barrier to see if they are the same as your pictures. Challenge older children by breaking words into three parts, eg **s – ui – t**, **s – ea – t**.

Tips

Help! The child keeps pointing to the wrong pictures! What can you do?

- This activity might be very new for the child. Help him get used to it, and reduce any pressure he might be feeling, by using a toy or a puppet. Follow the instructions with the toy or puppet, so that the child can watch and listen. When the toy or puppet points to a picture, say 'Hold on a minute'. Turn to the child and say, for example, '**S – afe**. Let's put them together, **s** [pause] **afe**. Safe! Did he point to the safe? He did, didn't he? Clever puppet! He got it right!' When the child is more familiar with the activity, the puppet or toy can start to make some mistakes. For example: you say '**s – afe**' and the puppet points to the picture of a seed. Check the puppet's answer with the child and see if he can help the puppet by pointing to the right picture (safe).

*Help! When the child tries to say longer words that begin with the speech sound **s**, eg **sun**, he says **t** (or **d**)! He says **tun** (or **dun**) instead of **sun**! What can you do?*

- This is primarily a listening activity, not a speaking activity. If the child points to the right picture, eg **sun**, you know that he has blended **s** and **un** together correctly in his head. The child said **tun** because he cannot say **s** in words yet. Say the word correctly for the child so that he has another opportunity to hear it, eg '**Sun**. [child repeats] Good work! You got it!'

*How can you help the child to say the speech sound **s** in words?*

Try a multi-sensory approach to make activities more memorable for children. In other words, make activities visual (use pictures, objects, Jolly Phonics gestures that help children remember sounds and letters, cued articulation – see Section 3); auditory (say the speech sound in words, phrases, sentences); tactile (involve movement if you can, for example touch word pictures, jump on word pictures).

- You will need two small objects, eg two coins, two Lego bricks, two toy cars, and small pictures of the words that you are working on with the child, eg **seat**, **sock**, **sun**, **sip**. Choose one of the pictures, eg **sip**. Put the two coins or Lego bricks or toy cars in front of the child, leaving a gap between the two objects. Touch the first object and say the first sound of the word: **s**. Then touch the second object and say the rest of the word, eg **ip** (**sip**). Take it in turns to touch the objects and say **s** and **ip** as you touch each one. Gradually move the two objects closer together so that the pause you leave between saying **s** and saying **ip** is smaller and smaller, until the objects are touching and there is no gap between **s** and **ip**, ie you are saying **sip**.

- Instead of asking the child to say **s – ip**, try asking him to say **si**, leave a pause and then say **p** (**si – p**). Saying a speech sound and doing a movement, eg touching a brick, touching one of your fingers, jumping on a mat, helps some children to say words. Use coins or bricks or toys as described in the first tip. Or try putting two mats or pieces of paper or lily pads or monsters' footprints on the floor for the child to step or jump on when he says **si** and **p**. Or try putting paper hands on a wall for the child to touch when he says **si** and **p**. Gradually bring the two mats or pieces of paper or hands together until they are touching and there is no gap between **si** and **p**, ie he is saying **sip**.

A or B? (Listening activity)

Aim
To help the child hear the difference between the speech sound he wants to say in words, **s**, and the speech sounds he is saying in words, eg **t** or **d**.

For example: she may want to say **sad**, but she says **dad**.

How?
By giving the child opportunities to hear, and see, you say short words that begin with **s** and short words that rhyme and start with **t** or **d** (depending on whether the child replaces **s** with **t** or with **d** in words).

Resources

- Large pictures of words that start with **s**: **save, sun, Sid, sock, sail, sum, sad, sell, sip, Sid, sad** (pp101–110)

- Pictures of words that start with **t** and rhyme with the words that start with **s**: **ton, tock, tail, tum, tell** (pp111–113).

- Pictures of words that start with **d** and rhyme with the words that start with **s**: **Dave, done, did, dock, Dale, dad, dip** (pp113–116).

- Pictures of lily pads or monsters' footprints (pp45–46).

- Playdough or Plasticine.

- Stickers.

Instructions

1. Choose a pair of words. For example: if the child says **t** instead of **s** in words, choose pairs of rhyming words that begin with **s** and begin with **t** (**sun** and **ton**, **sock** and **tock**, **sail** and **tail**, **sum** and **tum**, **sell** and **tell**).

   Photocopy the pictures and put them in front of the child.

2. Tell the child to listen carefully. Say the two words for him, eg '**Sail. Tail**'.

3. Give the child a sticker and ask him to listen again. Say one of the words, eg '**Sail**', and ask the child to put the sticker on the word he heard.

Note: See Section 3 for variations and tips for this activity.

My progress

Date	I can ...	☺/☹	I need to work on ...
	Listen carefully and hear words that begin with **s**, eg **sail**, **sun**, **sum**, without any help.		
	Listen carefully and hear words that begin with **s**, eg **sail**, **sun**, **sum**, with help.		
	Say **s** at the beginning of words, eg **sail**, **sun**, **sum**, without any help.		
	Say **s** at the beginning of words, eg **sail**, **sun**, **sum**, with some help.		

What's the next step?

- I can listen carefully and hear words that begin with **s**, eg **sail**, **sun**, **sum**, without any help. **Start doing listening activities in Section 5 (words that end with s, eg house, purse). Play listening games from the list of games in Section 9, eg Goal!, Listen and colour.**

- I can listen carefully and hear words that begin with **s**, eg **sail**, **sun**, **sum**, with help. **Carry on doing listening activities in Section 4. Use games from Section 3 and play listening games from the list of games in Section 9, eg Bowling, Catch a picture. When the child can hear words that begin with s in activities at least 70 per cent of the time, gradually introduce listening activities from Section 5.**

- I can say **s** at the beginning of words, eg **sail**, **sun**, **sum**, without any help. **Start working on Section 5. Play speaking games from the list of games in Section 9, eg Guess what?, What is it?**

- I can say **s** at the beginning of words, eg **sail**, **sun**, **sum**, with some help. **Carry on playing talking games from Section 4 and carry on doing mouth exercises from Section 1. Play games from the list of games in Section 9. When the child is able to say s at the beginning of longer words that begin with s without help at least 70 per cent of the time, gradually introduce speaking activities from Section 5.**

Look!

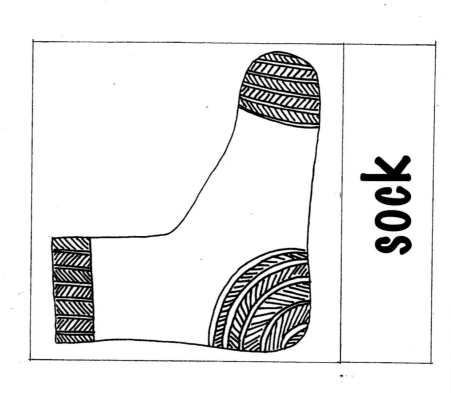

sock

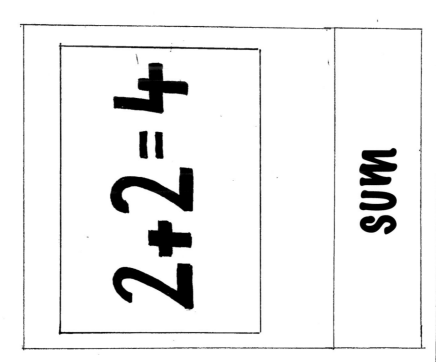

$$2 + 2 = 4$$

sum

seal

sack

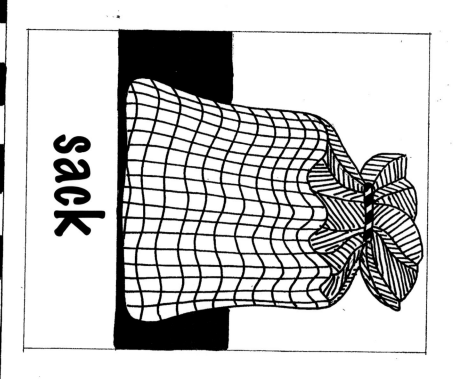

Look!

Look!

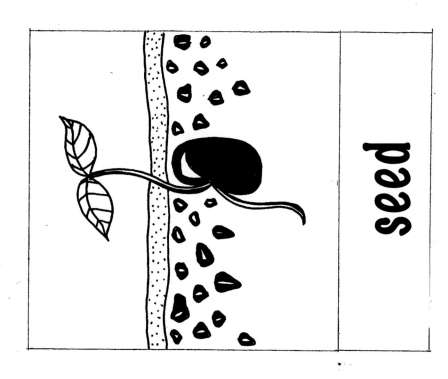

seed

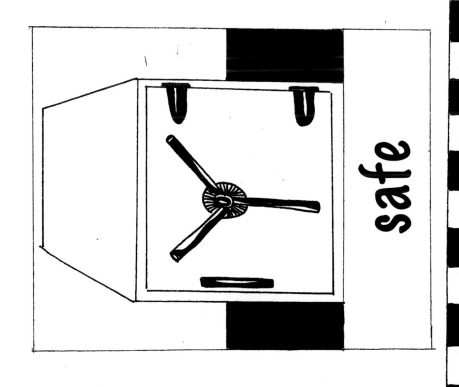

safe

sing

save

Look!

Look!

soup

soap

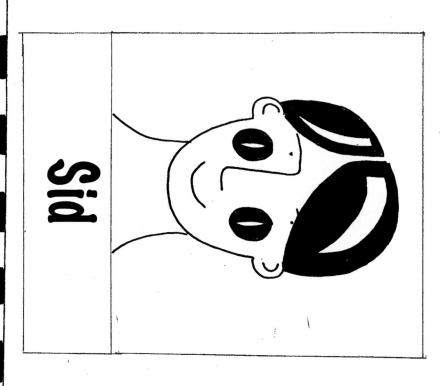

Sid

Sam

Look!

sword

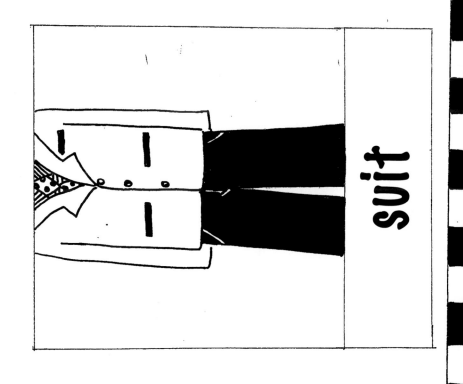

suit

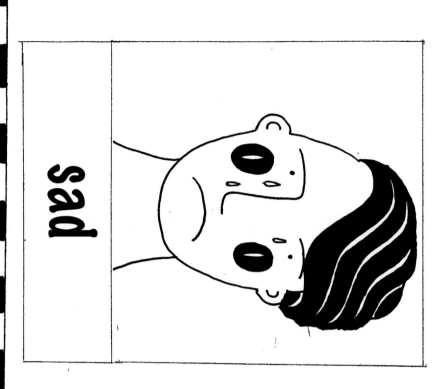

sad

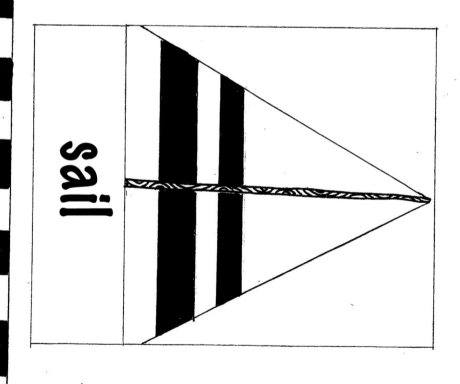

sail

look!

Look!

seat

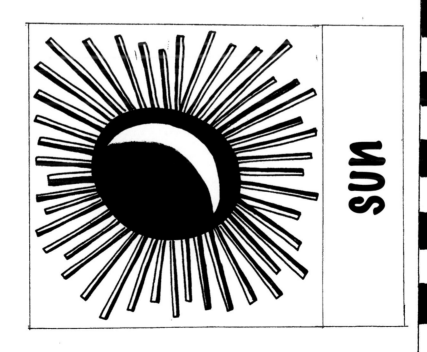

sun

Look!

sell

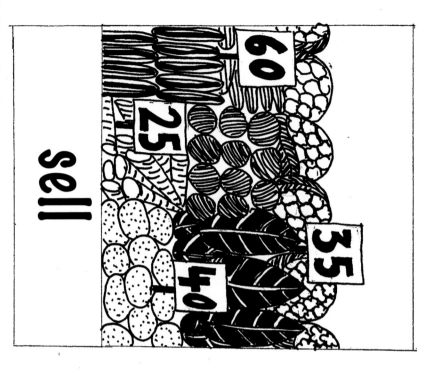

sip

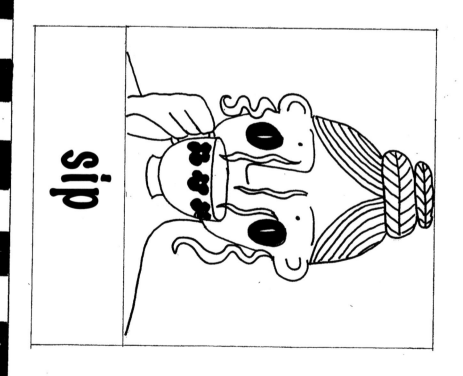

Look!

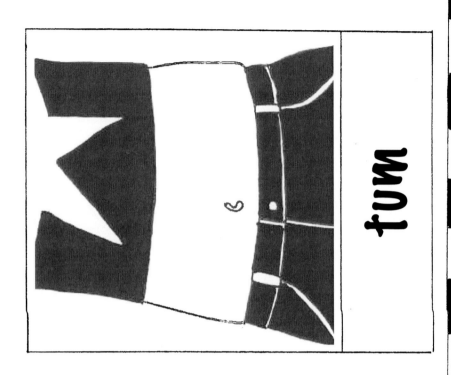

tum

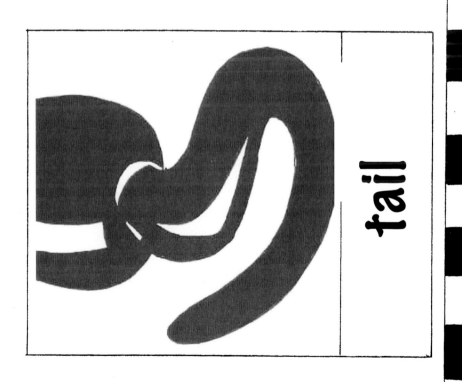

tail

ton

tock

look!

112

Look!

dave

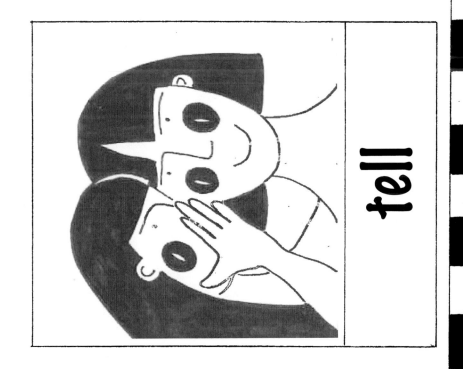

tell

Look!

did

done

Look!

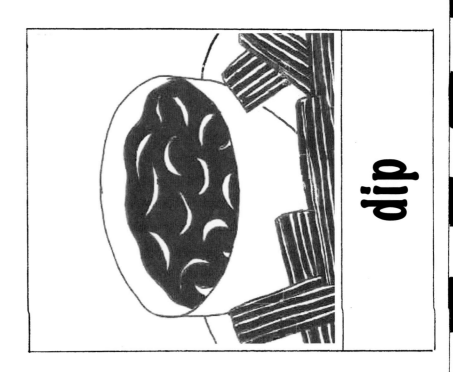

dip

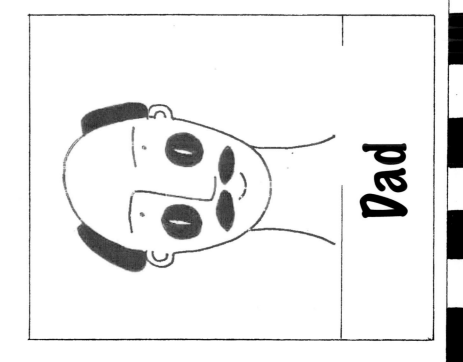

Dad

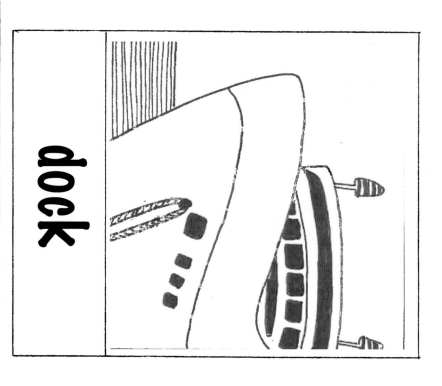

dock

Dale

Look!

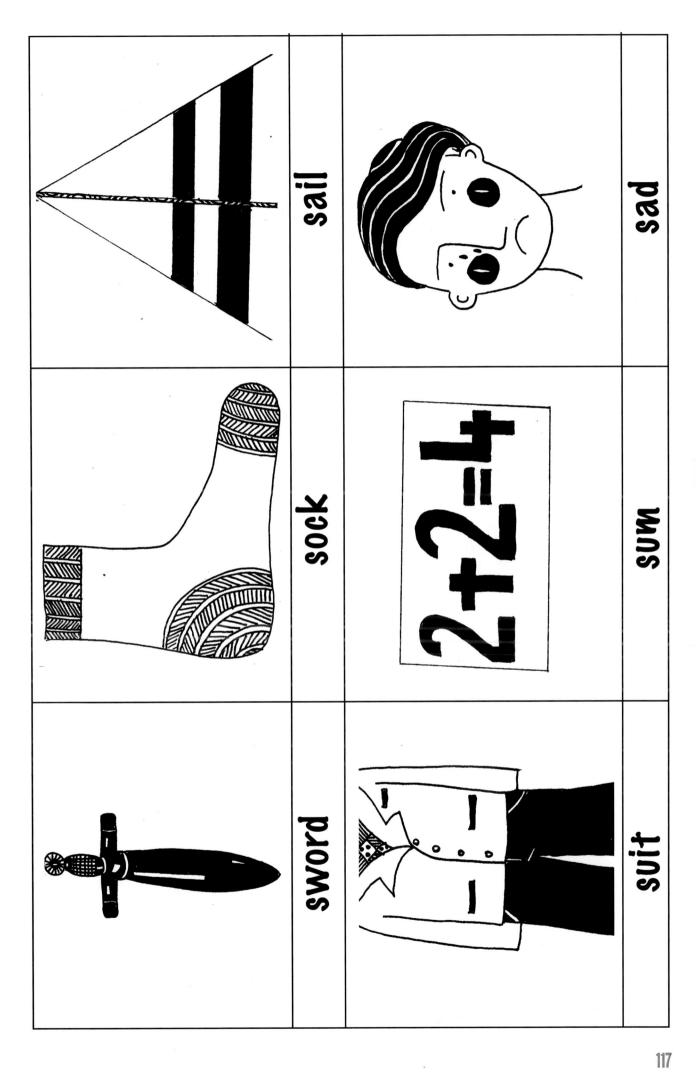

sail

sad

sock

sum

sword

suit

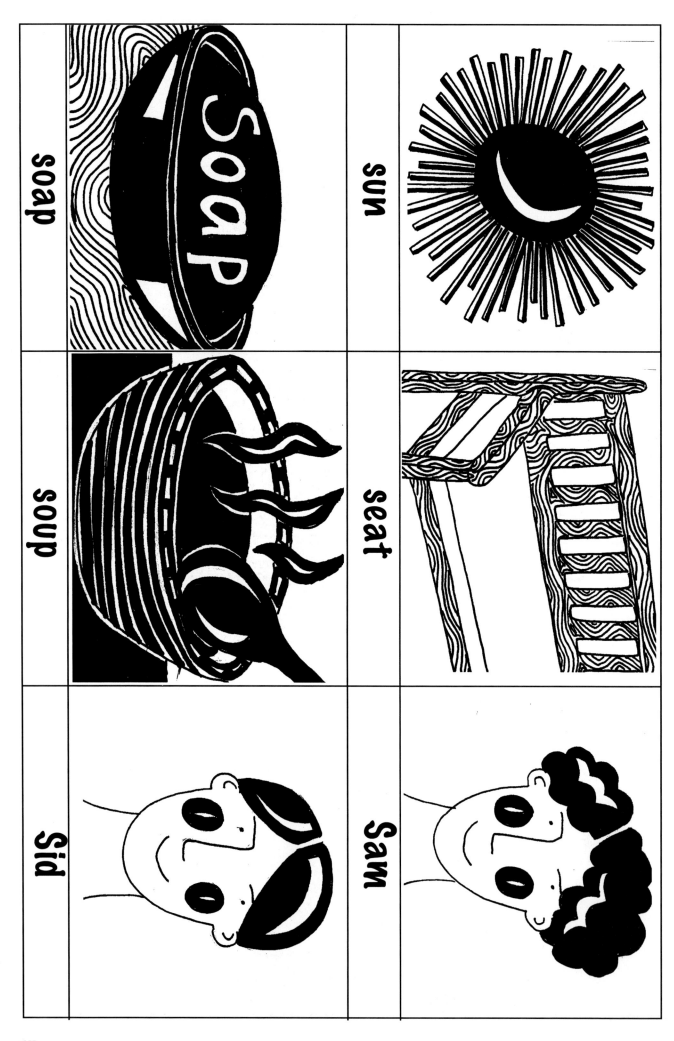

soap

sun

soup

seat

Sid

Sam

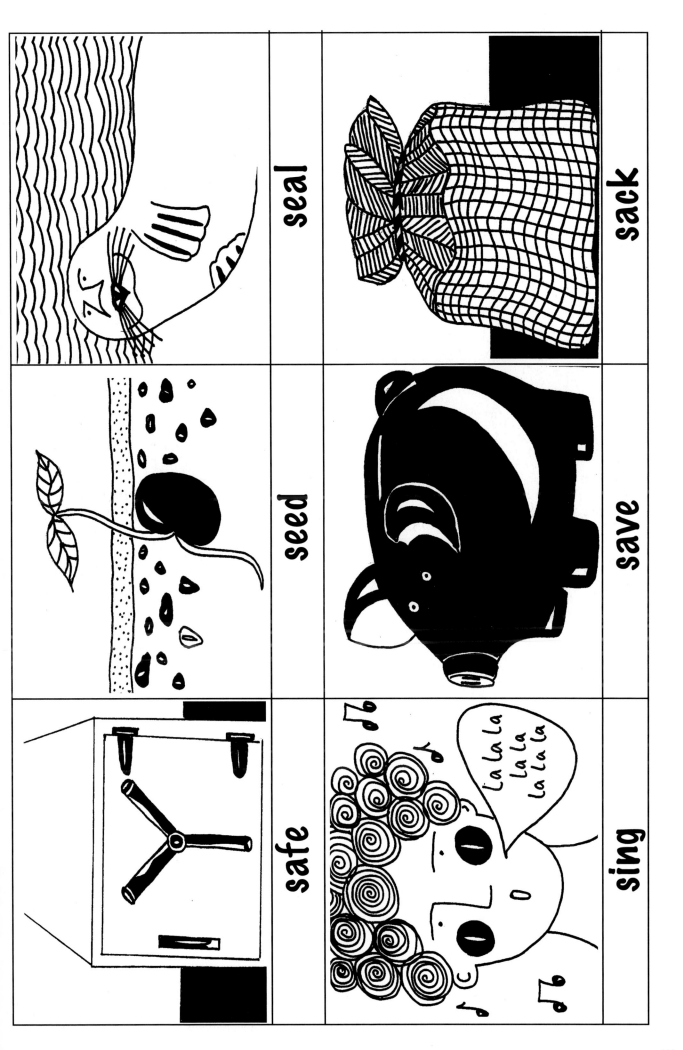

seal

sack

seed

save

safe

sing

sell

sip

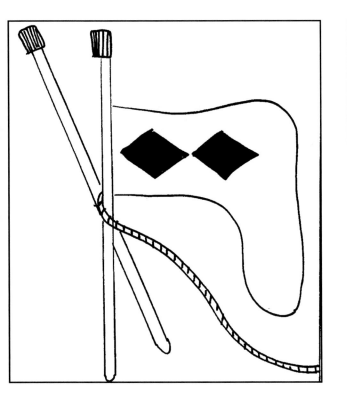
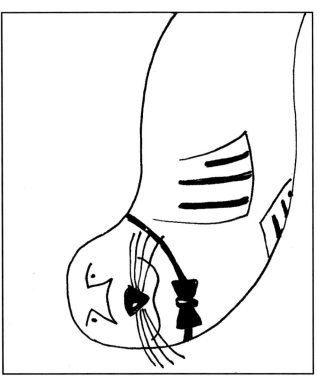

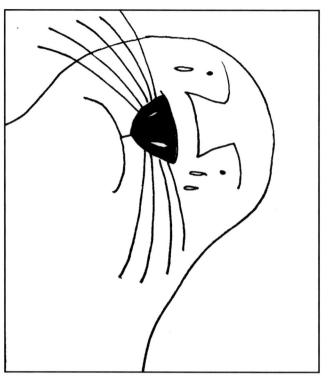

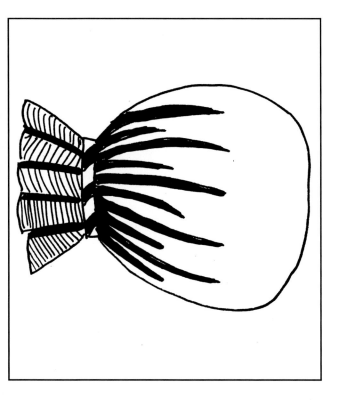

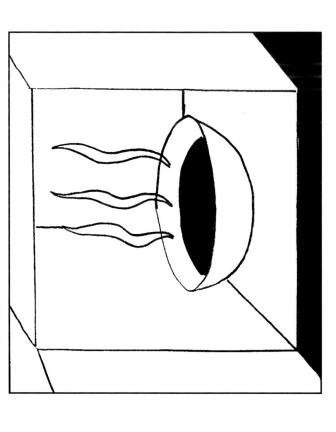

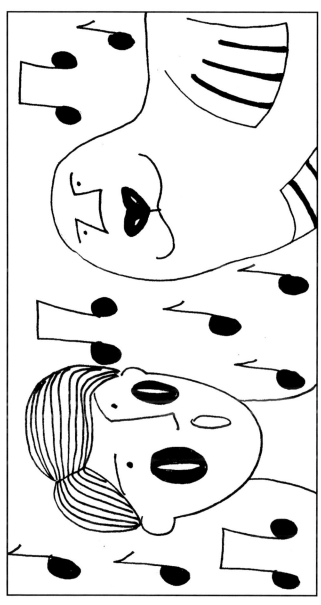

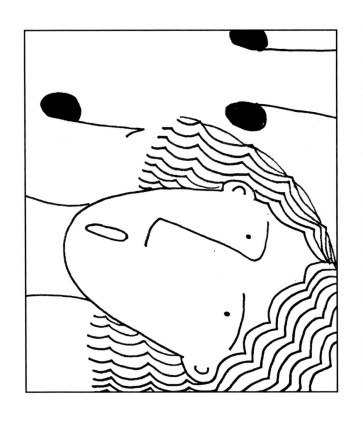

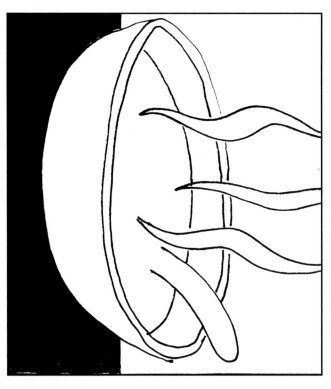

Jingles with words that begin with s

See advice at the end of Section 3 (p84) on how to use the jingles.

Jingle 1 (pictures on p121)

Listen

Ding dong

Sing a song

Tick tock

Knit a sock

Bee bop boot

Wear a suit

Pee po peel

Dance with a seal!

Say the word

Ding dong

Sing a _____ (song)

Tick tock

Knit a _____ (sock)

Bee bop boot

Wear a _____ (suit)

Pee po peel

Dance with a _____ (seal)!

Jingle 2 (pictures on p123)

Listen

Sam! Don't put your soup in the safe!

That would be silly!

Sam! Don't put your suit in a sack!

That would be silly!

Sam! Don't sing a song to a seal!

That would be the silliest!

Say the word

Sam! Don't put your _____ (soup) in the safe!

That would be silly!

Sam! Don't put your _____ (suit) in a sack!

That would be silly!

Sam! Don't sing a song to a _____ (seal)!

That would be the silliest!

Jingle 3 (pictures on p124)

Listen

What did you say?

I said sit on a seat

What did Sam say?

He said save me some soup

What did Sid say?

He said sing me a song

What did Seb say?

He said do NOT sing a song! Your singing is TERRIBLE!

Say the word

What did you _____ (say)?

I said sit on a _____ (seat)

What did _____ (Sam) say?

He said save me some _____ (soup)

What did _____ (Sid) say?

He said sing me a _____ (song)

What did _____ (Seb) say?

He said do NOT _____ (sing) a song! Your singing is TERRIBLE!

Jingle 4   (pictures on p122)

Listen

I saw a sad seal

Poor sad seal!

I saw a sad seal on a seat

Poor sad seal on a seat!

I saw a sad seal in a suit on a seat

Poor sad seal in a suit on a seat!

I saw a sad seal in a suit on a seat eating soup

I saw a ... Sorry! I can't remember all of that!

Say the word

I saw a sad _____ (seal)

Poor _____ (sad) seal!

I saw a sad seal on a _____ (seat)

Poor sad seal on a _____ (seat)!

I saw a sad seal in a _____ (suit) on a seat

Poor sad seal in a _____ (suit) on a seat!

I saw a sad seal in a suit on a seat eating _____ (soup)

I saw a ... Sorry! I can't remember allof that!

SECTION 5

SAYING S AT THE END OF LONGER WORDS

Section 5: Saying s at the end of longer words

What's the picture? (Speaking activity)

Aim

To say longer words that end with the speech sound **s**: **moose, dice, face, dress, bus, boss, house, goose, juice, rice, horse, dance, Miss, less, kiss, case, plus, six, purse, mouse, nurse, race**.

How?

By giving the child opportunities to hear, and see, you say longer words that end with **s** and to practise saying the words.

Resources

- Large pictures of longer words that end with **s** (pp140–150).

- Small pictures of longer words that end with **s** (pp151–154).

- Page of two doors with question marks on each one and the instruction *What's the picture?* (p81). You will need to photocopy this page and laminate it, then cut along three sides of the doors so that you can open them to reveal a picture.

- The page of emotions (p31), eg *happy, sad, angry*. You will need to photocopy this page and cut it into cards.

Instructions

1. Put the page with the doors on top of a page of large pictures of words that end with **s**, eg **bus** and **face**.

2. Read the instruction at the top of the page to the child: *What's the picture? Open the door and see.* Before you open the door to see what the picture is, say 'My turn!' so that the child knows you are going first. Open the first door to reveal the picture and name it, eg 'Look! **Bus**!', so that the child has an opportunity to hear you say **s** at the end of the word.

3. When you have finished your go, say to the child 'Your turn!' so that she knows that it is her go to open the door and name the picture behind it.

4. Put the picture of the doors over a different page of large pictures, eg **bus** and **face**, and take it in turns to open a door and name the picture behind it.

Follow this procedure to name all the pictures on the pages for this activity.

Variation

Put the laminated doors over two large pictures. Ask the child to guess what the picture is before she opens the door to see. For example: 'What do you think the picture is? I think it is the **juice**.' Tell the child to close her eyes and put a small picture behind each door. Then ask her to open her eyes and open the doors, but to guess what the picture is before she opens the door.

Note: See advice in Section 3 for helping children to say **s** in words.

Roll and say (Speaking activity)

Aim

To say longer words that end with the speech sound **s**: **moose, dice, face, dress, bus, boss, house, goose, juice, rice, horse, dance, Miss, less, kiss, case, plus, six, purse, mouse, nurse, race.**

How?

By giving the child opportunities to hear, and see, you say words that end with **s** and to practise saying the words.

Resources

- A set of six small pictures (pp151–154) with shapes on the back, cut up and laminated (photocopy the sheet of shapes (p83) on to the back of the pictures so that they are double sided).

- A dice.

- Template for a dice with a different shape on each face (p30).

Instructions

1. Spread the pictures out in front of the child, face down so that you can see the shapes on the back.

2. Roll the dice with shapes on it. The shapes on the dice match the shapes on the back of the pictures. Turn over the picture that has the same shape as the dice, eg circle, so that you can see what the picture is, eg **bus**.

3. Roll the dice with numbers on it. You have to say the word on your picture, eg **bus**, the number of times that you throw on the dice, eg 5: '**bus, bus, bus, bus, bus**'. Make sure you have the first turn so that you can demonstrate the activity to the child.

Variations

- Make the game competitive: the winner is the first person to say the names of all of the six pictures in the activity, ie to throw all of the shapes on the dice.

- Roll the dice with shapes on it and turn over the picture that has the same shape on it, eg heart. Take it in turns to see how many times you can say the word in a minute. Use a one-minute salt timer.

Remember and say (Listening and speaking activity)

Aim

To say longer words that end with the speech sound **s: moose, dice, face, dress, bus, boss, house, goose, juice, rice, horse, dance, Miss, less, kiss, case, plus, six, purse, mouse, nurse, race**.

How?

By giving the child opportunities to hear, and see, you say words that end with **s** and to practise saying the words.

Resources

- At least one set of the small pictures of words that end with **s** (pp151–154).

Instructions

1. Look at the pictures of the words that end with **s** and name them with the child (see tips in Sections 3 and 4 on choosing how many and which pictures to present to children).

2. Present at least two of the pictures to the child and name them, eg '**Bus. Dice**'. Tell the child to 'take a photo' of the pictures in her mind, ie use a mental camera, to help her remember them. Give her at least 30 seconds to look at the pictures. Then turn them over and ask the child if she can remember what they are. The child then names the pictures.

   Turn them over to see if she is right. Make this activity more challenging by increasing the number of pictures that the child has to remember.

Note: See Section 4 for variations of this activity.

Listen and guess (Listening and speaking activity)

Aim

To say longer words that end with the speech sound **s**: **moose**, **dice**, **face**, **dress**, **bus**, **boss**, **house**, **goose**, **juice**, **rice**, **horse**, **dance**, **Miss**, **less**, **kiss**, **case**, **plus**, **six**, **purse**, **mouse**, **nurse**, **race**.

How?

By giving the child opportunities to hear, and see, you say words that end with **s** and to practise saying the words.

Resources

- Two sets of the small pictures of words that end with **s** (pp151–154).

Instructions

1. Choose a picture, eg **purse.** Do not show it to the child. Place it face down in front of her.

2. Tell the child at least three things about the picture, eg 'It is small. It is often made of leather. You keep money in it.'

3. The child guesses what the picture is and turns it over to see if she is right. Reverse the game so that the child chooses a picture and describes it and you guess what it is.

Variations

- To make this activity less challenging for the child, put at least three pictures in front of her, eg **bus**, **horse**, **case**. Choose one of the pictures to describe, eg **horse**. Do not tell the child which one you have chosen. Tell her three things about the picture, eg 'It's an animal. It has four legs and a tail. You can ride it.' The child listens and points to the picture that she thinks you are describing, eg **horse**.

- To make this activity more challenging, choose at least three pictures. Do not show them to the child. Place them face down in front of her. Tell the child at least three things about the first picture. The child guesses what it is and turns it over to see if she is correct. Then tell her three things about the second picture. The child guesses and checks if she is right or not. Follow the same procedure for the third picture. Reverse the game, so that the child chooses at least three pictures and describes them to you.

- Place a barrier between you and the child. Make sure that you each have a set of the small pictures. Choose at least three pictures from your set, eg **rice**, **juice**, **moose**.

Describe the pictures to the child, leaving a pause between each description so that she can find the one she thinks you are talking about in her set. When the child has found the picture she thinks you are describing, she puts it face up behind the barrier so that you cannot see it. When you have described all three pictures and the child has put three corresponding pictures behind the barrier, ask her to say what her pictures are, eg '**rice, juice, moose**'. Then remove the barrier to see if she has the same pictures as you. Reverse the game, so that the child chooses and describes three pictures and you listen.

What did I say? (Listening and speaking activity)

Aim

To say longer words that end with the speech sound **s: moose, dice, face, dress, bus, boss, house, goose, juice, rice, horse, dance, Miss, less, kiss, case, plus, six, purse, mouse, nurse, race**.

How?

By giving the child opportunities to hear, and see, you say longer words that end with **s** and to practise saying the words.

Resources

- At least two sets of the small pictures of words that end with **s** (pp151–154).

Instructions

You are the speaker and the child is the listener in these activities.

1. Choose two pictures, eg **dress** and **nurse**. Put them on the table in front of the child and name them for her: '**Dress. Nurse**'. Tell the child to listen carefully and then you name one of the pictures placed in front of her, eg '**Nurse**'. Then say 'What did I say?' The child listens and points to, or holds up, or puts a counter on the word she heard you say.

2. When you think the child is ready to listen and remember more words, choose three pictures, eg **nurse, dress** and **face**. Put them on the table in front of the child and name them for her: '**Nurse. Dress. Face**'. Tell the child to listen carefully and then you name two of the pictures placed in front of her, eg '**Nurse. Face**'. Then say 'What did I say?' The child listens and points to, or holds up, or puts a counter on the words she heard you say. Increase the number of words to make the activity more challenging when you think the child is ready.

Note: See variations and tips for this activity in Section 3.

What's the word? (Listening activity)

Aim
To say longer words that end with the speech sound **s**: **moose**, **dice**, **face**, **dress**, **bus**, **boss**, **house**, **goose**, **juice**, **rice**, **horse**, **dance**, **Miss**, **less**, **kiss**, **case**, **plus**, **six**, **purse**, **mouse**, **nurse**, **race**.

How?
By giving the child opportunities to hear, and see, you say words that end with **s** and to practise saying the words.

Resources
- At least two sets of the small pictures of words that end with **s** (pp151–154).

Instructions
This activity is for children aged four and a half upwards.

1. Lay a set of the small pictures in front of the child. Name them with her, so that she can hear the words before you start the activity.

Tips
- Use at least three small pictures with younger children. Be flexible with the number of pictures you present at the beginning of the activity depending on the level of the child.

- The aim of this activity is to help the child say **s** at the end of words. Some children may have other speech sound difficulties. For example, they may say **w** instead of **r** in words (**wice** instead of **rice**). However, you are working on saying **s** in words, so this is the only speech sound you need to focus on in these activities.

2. Tell the child to listen carefully and point to the picture you are naming. Break words into two parts, eg 'bo – ss'. Leave a short pause between the speech sounds to help the child carry out this task. The child has to put the speech sounds together in her head to make the word, eg **boss**, and then point to the picture of a boss.

3. When the child is familiar with this activity, ask her to put the sounds together silently in her head, point to the picture and say the word out loud, eg '**boss**'.

Note: See Section 3 for ideas for variations of this activity which you can play with the words in Section 5.

Tip

How can I help the child to say s at the end of words?

You will need two small objects, eg two coins, two Lego bricks, two toy cars, and small pictures of the words that you are working on with the child, eg **purse**, **nurse**, **bus**. Choose one of the pictures, eg **bus**. Put the two coins or Lego bricks or toy cars in front of the child, leaving a gap between the two objects. Touch the first object and say the first part of the word, eg **bu**. Then touch the second object and say the final speech sound, **s** (**bu – s**). Take it in turns to touch the coins/bricks/cars and say **bu** and **s** as you touch each one. Gradually move the two objects closer together so that the pause you leave between saying **bu** and saying **s** is smaller and smaller, until the coins/bricks/cars are touching and there is no gap between **bu** and **s**, ie you are saying **bus**.

Odd one out (Listening and speaking activity)

Aim

To say longer words that end with the speech sound **s**: **moose**, **dice**, **face**, **dress**, **bus**, **boss**, **house**, **goose**, **juice**, **rice**, **horse**, **dance**, **Miss**, **less**, **kiss**, **case**, **plus**, **six**, **purse**, **mouse**, **nurse**, **race**.

How?

By giving the child opportunities to hear, and see, you say words that end with **s** and to practise saying the words.

Resources

- A set of the small pictures of words that end with **s** (pp151–154).

Instructions

1. See the grid below (p138) for suggestions for pictures for this activity, eg **horse**, **mouse**, **goose**. Put the three pictures in front of the child.

2. Name the pictures for the child, '**Horse. Mouse. Goose**', and ask 'Which one do you think is different?'

Tip

If the child is not able to select one, or is finding it hard to think why one is different from the other two, help her by giving her clues. For example: 'Let's have a think together. How many legs has a horse got? That's right, four. What about a moose? How many legs has a moose got? Yes, that's got four legs too, hasn't it? OK, what about a goose? How many legs has a goose got? Two. So a horse has four legs, a moose has four legs and a goose has two legs. Have they all the same number of legs? No, they haven't, have they? Which one is different? That's right, the goose because that's only got two legs, hasn't it? So which one is the odd one out?'

Odd one out

Which is the odd one out?			Possible answer
Horse	Goose	Bus	**Bus** because it is not an animal.
Goose	Horse	Mouse	**Goose** because it has two legs and a horse and a mouse have four legs.
Plus	Rice	Less	**Rice** because it is a food, not a word used in maths.
Mouse	Boss	Nurse	**Mouse** because it is an animal and the others are people.
Dance	Purse	Case	**Dance** because you can put things in a purse and a case but you can't put things in dance.

My progress

Date	I can ...	☺/☹	I need to work on ...
	Listen carefully and hear words that end with **s**, eg **bus**, **purse**, **horse**, without any help.		
	Listen carefully and hear words that end with **s**, eg **bus**, **purse**, **horse**, with help.		
	Say **s** at the end of words, eg **bus**, **purse**, **horse**, without any help.		
	Say **s** at the end of words, eg **bus**, **purse**, **horse**, with some help.		

What's the next step?

- I can listen carefully and hear words that end with **s**, eg **bus**, **purse**, **horse**, without any help. **Continue to play listening games from the list of games in Section 9 (p261). Start working on Section 6.**

- I can listen carefully and hear words that end with **s**, eg **bus**, **purse**, **horse**, with help. **Continue playing listening games from Section 5. Play listening games from earlier sections to revise listening to s in words and listening games from the list of games in Section 9, eg Listen and do. When the child can hear words that end with s 70 per cent of the time in listening games, start working on listening games in Section 6.**

- I can say **s** at the end of words, eg **bus**, **purse**, **horse**, without any help. **Start working on speaking activities in Section 6. Play speaking games from the list of games at the back of the resource, eg Pairs, Kim's game.**

- I can say **s** at the end of words, eg **bus**, **purse**, **horse**, with some help. **Continue doing speaking activities from Section 5. Play speaking games from the list of games in Section 9 (p261). When the child can say words that end with s 70 per cent of the time in speaking games, start working on listening games in Section 6.**

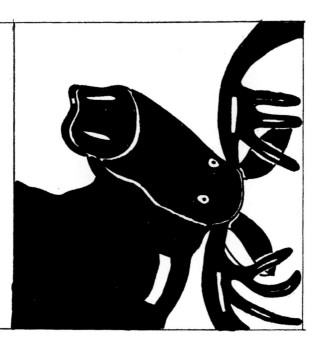

moose

dress

Look!

Look!

face

bus

boss

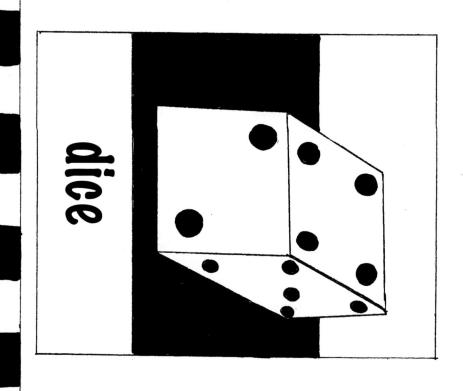

dice

Look!

Look!

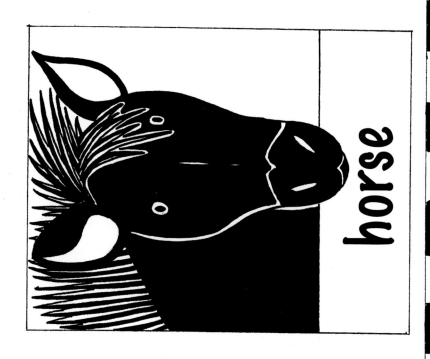

horse

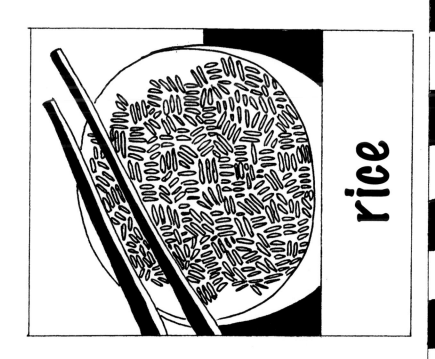

rice

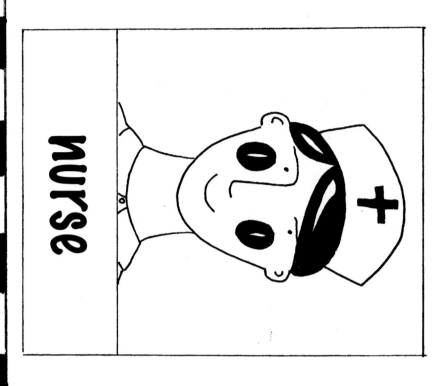

nurse

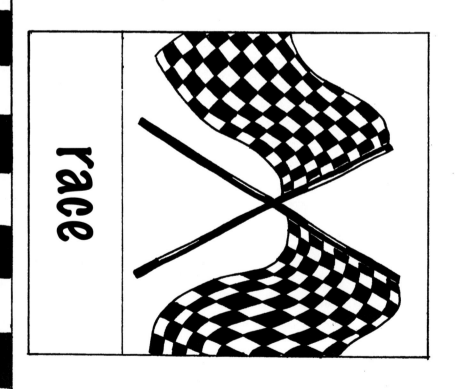

race

Look!

Look!

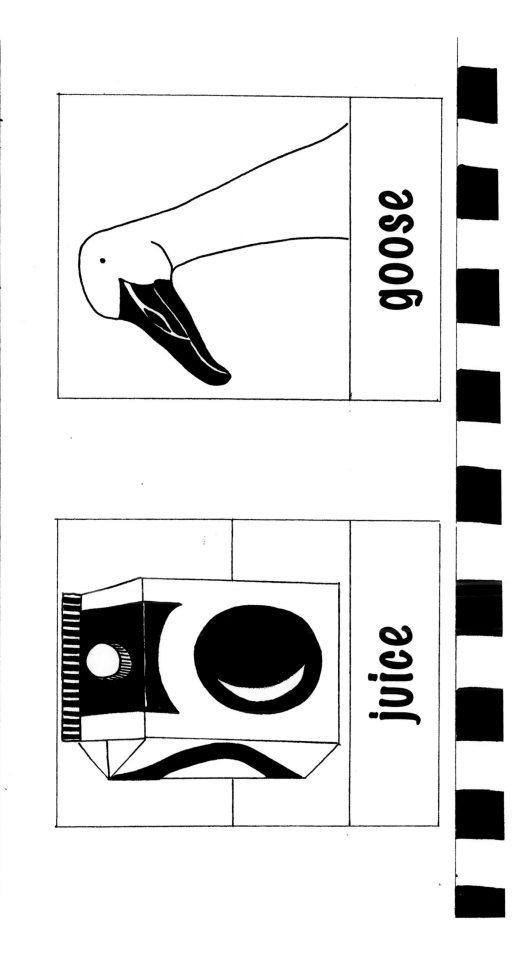

goose

juice

Look!

dance

house

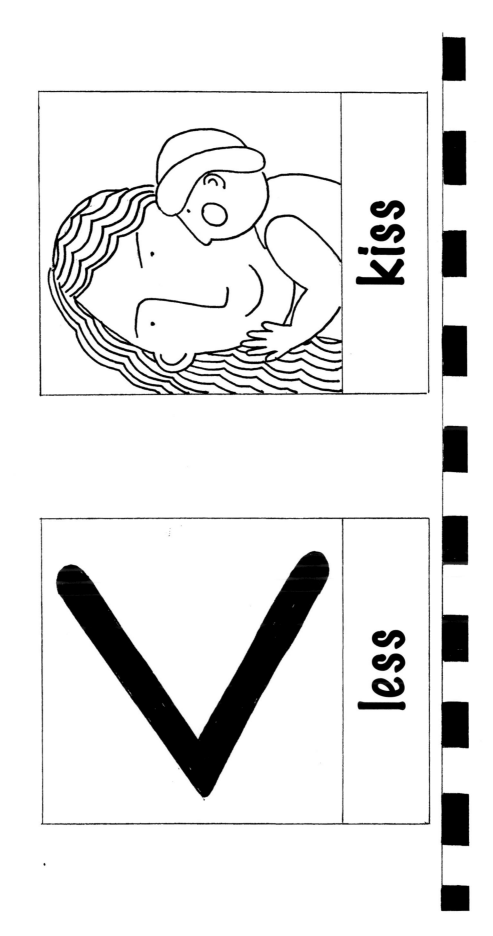

look!

kiss

less

Look!

Miss

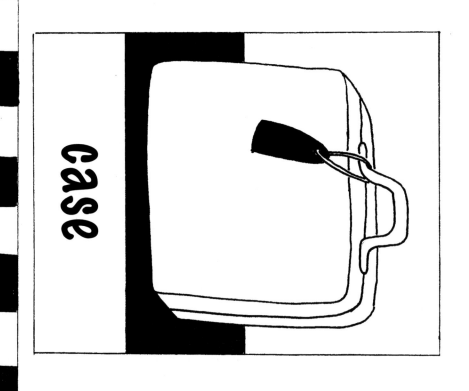

case

Look!

purse

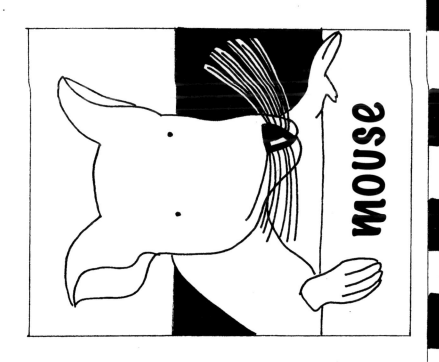

mouse

look!

plus

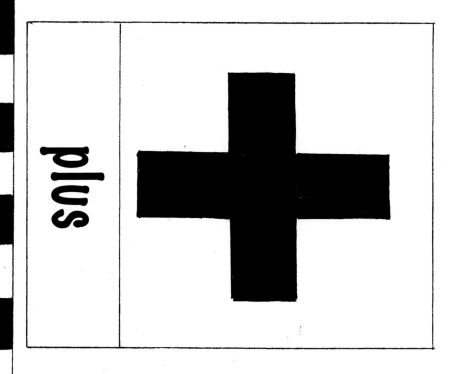

six

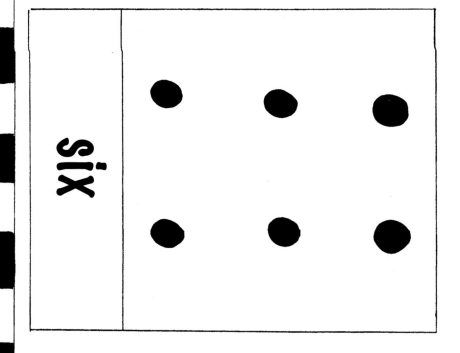

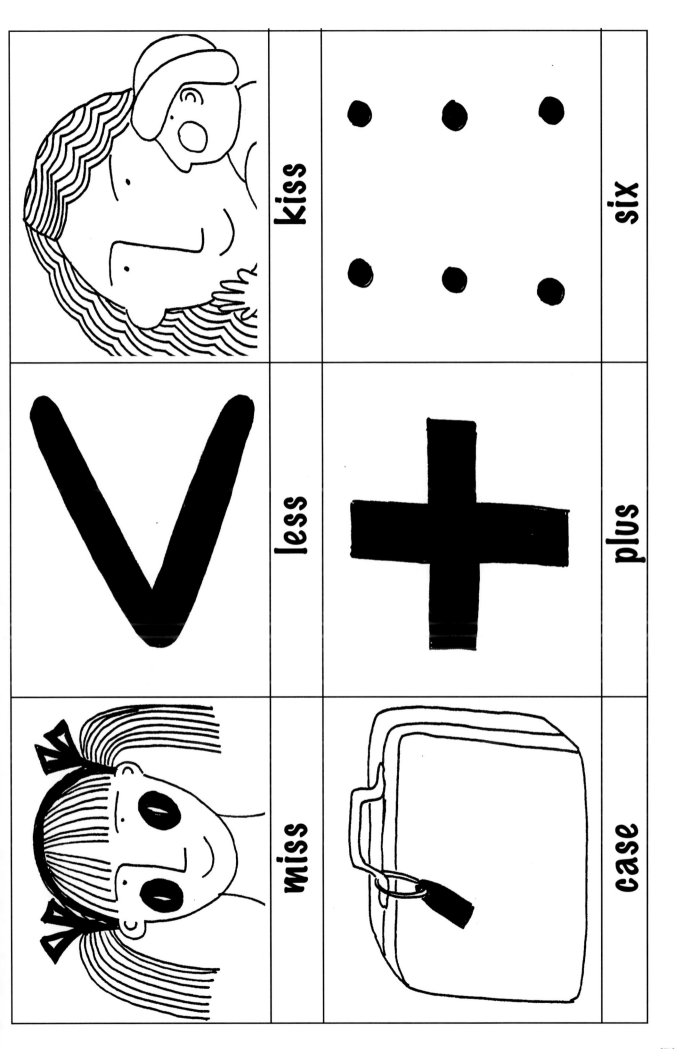

kiss

six

less

plus

miss

case

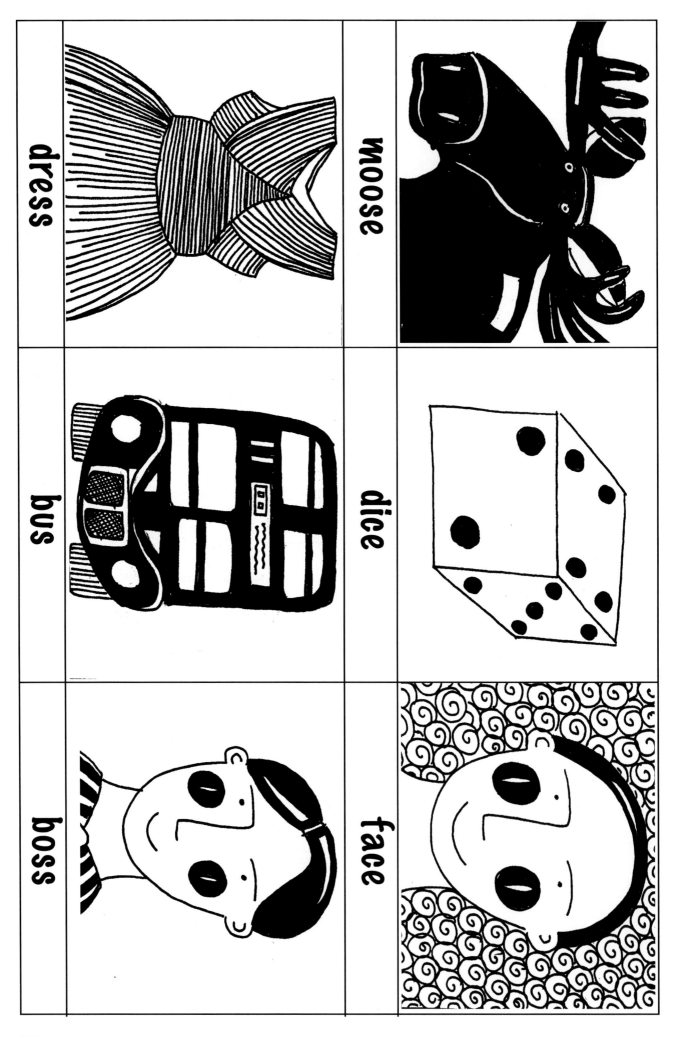

dress

moose

bus

dice

boss

face

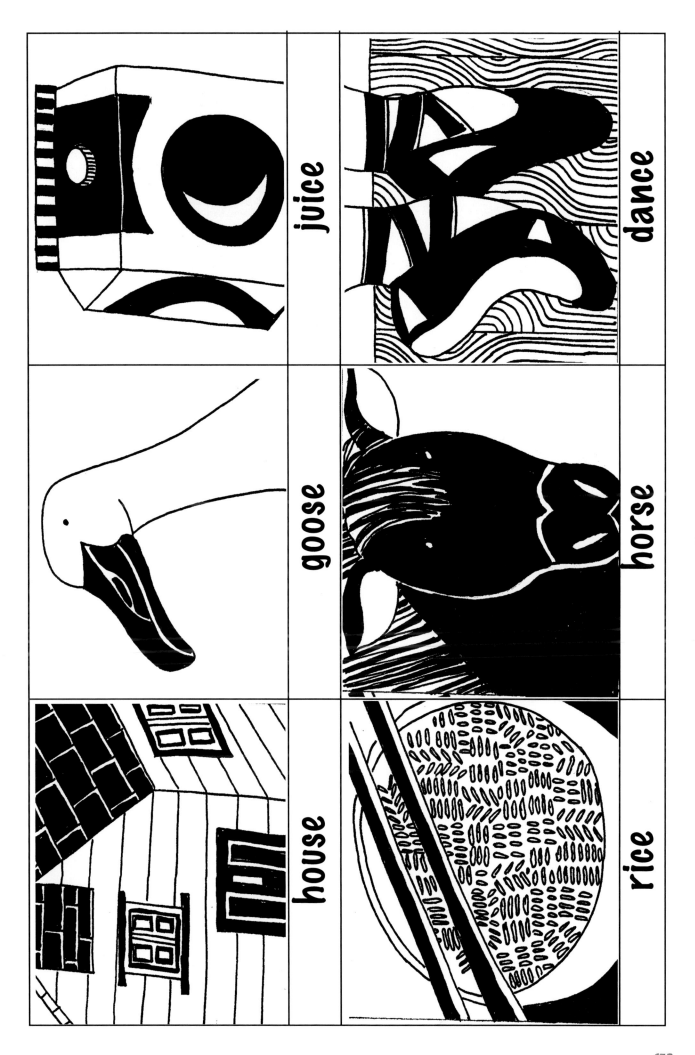

juice

dance

goose

horse

house

rice

purse

mouse

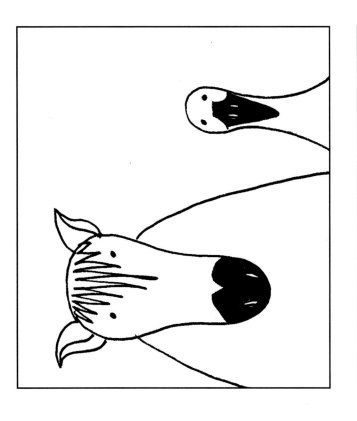

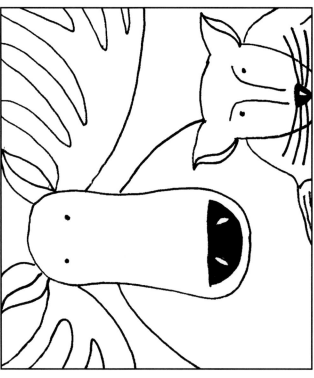

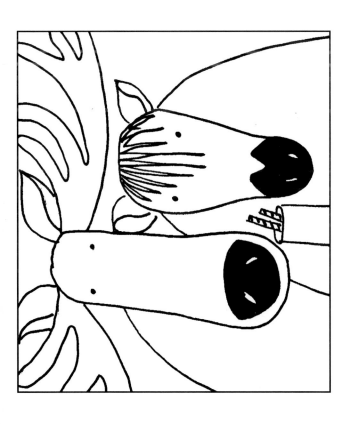

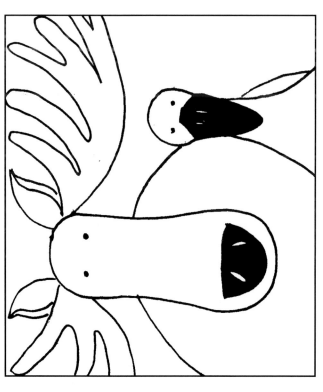

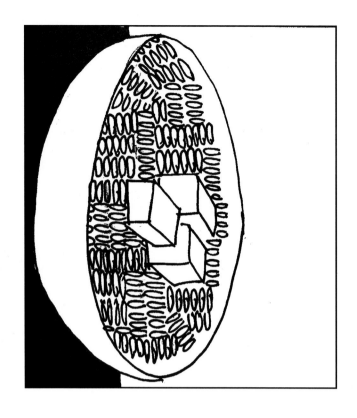

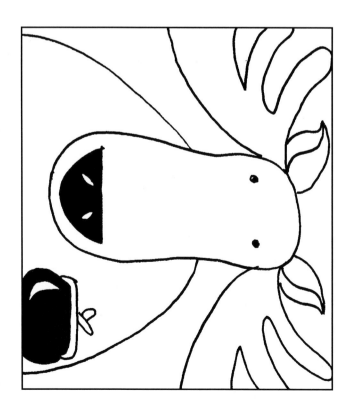

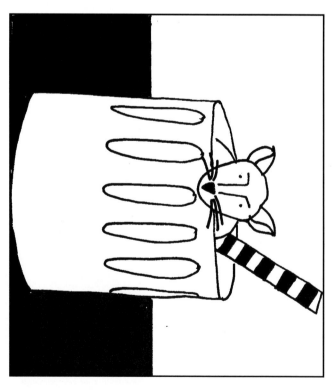

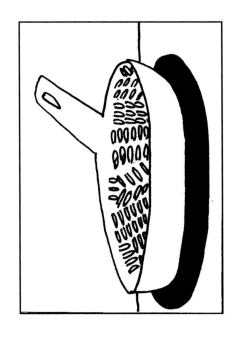
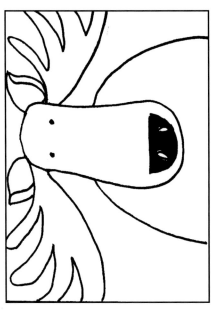
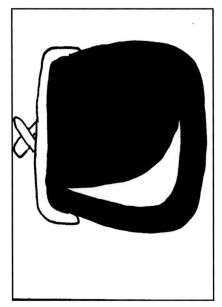

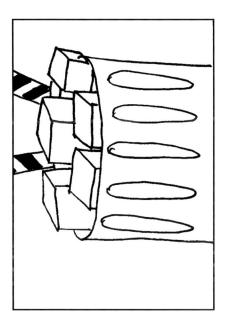
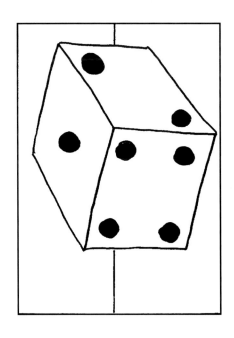
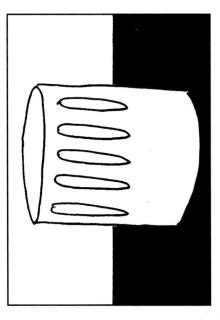

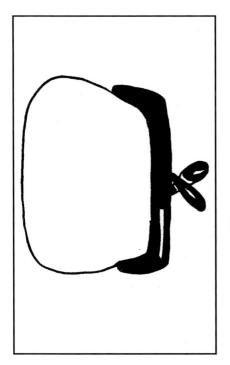
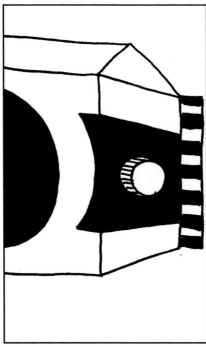

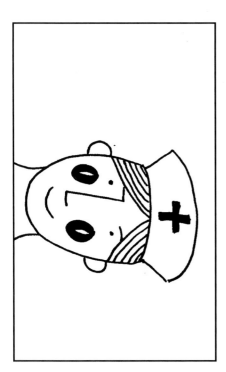
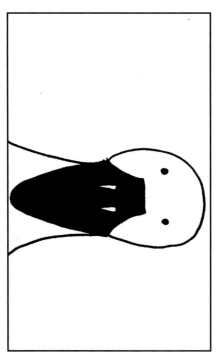
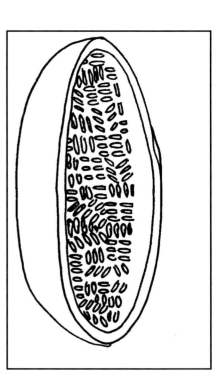

Jingles with words that end with s

See advice at the end of Section 3 (pp84–85) on how to use the jingles.

Jingle 1   (pictures on p155)

Listen

Would you rather share your juice with a mouse or a horse?

Would you rather dance with a horse or a goose?

Would you rather race a goose or a moose?

Would you rather kiss a moose or a mouse?

I would rather just go home!

Say the word

Would you rather share your juice with a mouse or a _____ (horse)?

Would you rather dance with a horse or a _____ (goose)?

Would you rather race a goose or a _____ (moose)?

Would you rather kiss a moose or a _____ (mouse)?

I would rather just go home!

Jingle 2   (pictures on p156)

Listen

Help! There's a mouse in the house!

Help! There's a mouse drinking my juice!

Help! There's some ice in my rice!

Help! A moose stole my purse!

I am having a VERY bad day!

Say the word

Help! There's a mouse in the _____ (house)!

Help! There's a mouse drinking my _____ (juice)!

Help! There's some ice in my _____ (rice)!

Help! A moose stole my _____ (purse)!

I am having a VERY bad day!

Jingle 3 (pictures on p157)

Listen

Bee by bice

Roll a dice

Catch a bus

Fry some rice

Bee by boose

Drink a juice

Wash your face

Chase a moose

Bee by burse

Telephone a nurse

Get a drink with ice

Count the money in your purse

Bee by bice

Say the word

Bee by _____ (bice)

Roll a _____ (dice)

Catch a _____ (bus)

Fry some _____ (rice)

Bee by _____ (boose)

Drink a _____ (juice)

Wash your _____ (face)

Chase a _____ (moose)

Bee by _____ (burse)

Telephone a _____ (nurse)

Get a drink with _____ (ice)

Count the money in your _____ (purse)

Bee by _____ (bice)

Jingle 4   (pictures on p158)

Listen

Dee diddly dice

Pass me the ice

Pass you the rice?

No! Pass me the ice!

Dee diddly doose

Pass me the juice

Pass you the goose?

No! Pass me the juice!

Dee diddly durse

Pass me my purse

Pass you a nurse?

No! Pass me my purse!

Dee diddly dase

Pass me my case

Dee diddly delf

Get it yourself!

Say the word

Dee diddly _____ (dice)

Pass me the _____ (ice)

Pass you the _____ (rice)?

No! Pass me the _____ (ice)!

Dee diddly _____ (doose)

Pass me the _____ (juice)

Pass you the _____ (goose)?

No! Pass me the _____ (juice)!

Dee diddly _____ (durse)

Pass me my _____ (purse)

Pass you a _____ (nurse)?

No! Pass me my _____ (purse)!

Dee diddly _____ (dase)

Pass me my _____ (case)

Dee diddly _____ (delf)

Get it yourself!

Jingle 5   (see the picture of a bus on p141)

Listen

Here comes the bus!

Quick! Run for it!

Hurry! Chase it!

Faster! Race it!

Don't miss it! You'll be late for school!

Say the word

Here comes the _____ (bus)!

Quick! Run for it!

Hurry! _____ (Chase) it!

Faster! _____ (Race) it!

Don't _____ (miss) it! You'll be late for school!

SAYING S IN WORDS WITH MORE THAN ONE SYLLABLE

Section 6: Saying s in words with more than one syllable

Look and guess (Speaking activity)

Aim

To say longer words that contain the speech sound **s: sandal, sardine, soldier, surgeon, princess, seagull, minus, seven, delicious, police, Santa, dangerous, surfboard, sunny, salad, city, seaweed, salt, cinema, sausage, saddle, sofa, cereal, sandwich, furious, waitress, saucepan, tennis, scissors, curious, sixteen, sixty, sailor, seventeen, seventy, circle, octopus, sauce, singer, necklace.**

How?

By giving the child opportunities to hear, and see, you say longer words that contain **s** and to practise saying the words.

Resources

- Two pictures of magnifying glasses (p173). Each magnifying glass has a hole in the lens. Cut out each magnifying glass and cut the hole out on each one.

- Large pictures of longer words that contain **s** (pp174–193).

Instructions

1. Make sure the child cannot see the pictures. Cover one of the pictures with the magnifying glass that has the smaller hole so that a bit of the picture can be seen through the hole.

2. Let the child have two or three guesses at what the picture is. If he cannot guess, change magnifying glasses so that the hole in the lens is bigger and more of the picture can be seen through it. Ask the child what he thinks the picture is.

Variations

Put the laminated doors (p81) on top of the page so that the pictures are covered. Take it in turns to open the doors and name the pictures.

Tips

*Help! The child says **t** (or **d**) instead of **s** in longer words! He says **tennit** instead of **tennis**! What can you do?*

Break the word into two halves, eg **te** and **nnis**. Leave a pause between the two halves, eg **te** (pause) **nnis**. Gradually make the pause that you leave between the two halves of the word smaller until there is no pause and you are saying the word: '**tennis**'. Try some of the ideas described in the tips to help a child say longer words that start with **s** (Section 4, p96). For example: put two paper hands on the wall. Touch a hand and say **te**. Touch the other hand and say **nnis**. Gradually bring the hands closer together, making the pause between **te** and **nnis** smaller. When the child is ready, put the hands next to each other and say the word without a pause: '**tennis**'. Exaggerate **sssss** to help the child hear the difference between **t** and **s**.

*Help! You have tried these tips and the child still finds it hard to say longer words! He gets all the sounds muddled up and doesn't say all the sounds in words! He says **lice** for **police**! What can you do?*

It takes some children longer than others to say words. Children need to hear words many times in order to say them correctly. They need lots of opportunities to practise saying the words you are working on in activities and games. Regular repetition is important. Carry out work at the child's pace. Help children to hear all the sounds in words and raise their awareness of how long words are by counting the syllables in words you are working on, eg **ci – ty** (two syllables), **de – li – cious** (three syllables). Say the word, so that the child can hear it, and clap the syllables at the same time. Ask the child to say it and clap it with you. Say it with the child and stamp the syllables or tap the syllables with a pencil or your finger. Count the syllables on your fingers with the child so that he can see how many syllables words have.

Finish my word (Speaking activity)

Aim

To say longer words that contain the speech sound **s**: **sandal, sardine, soldier, surgeon, princess, seagull, minus, seven, delicious, police, Santa, dangerous, surfboard, sunny, salad, city, seaweed, salt, cinema, sausage, saddle, sofa, cereal, sandwich, furious, waitress, saucepan, tennis, scissors, curious, sixteen, sixty, sailor, seventeen, seventy, circle, octopus, sauce, singer, necklace.**

How?

By giving the child opportunities to hear, and see, you say longer words that contain **s** and to practise saying the words.

Resources

- Two sets of the small pictures of longer words that contain **s** (pp194–199).

Instructions

This activity is for children aged four and a half upwards.

1. Put at least three pictures in a line in front of the child, eg **circle**, **scissors**, **sunny**. Tell the child that you have a really bad memory and can't remember the ends of words. Ask the child if he can help you name the pictures.

2. Say the first syllable of each word, eg '**Cir**_____. Oh, what is it? **Cir** _____. I know it, I just can't quite remember it! **Cir**____ It's no good, I can't remember it! Can you help me?' See if the child can complete the word (**circle**). If they say '**cle**', say the word aloud, eg '**Circle**! Of course! Thanks' and then ask them to say it for you, eg 'Oh, no! I've forgotten it again! Can you help me again, please! What is it?'

Variations

- Put at least three pictures in front of the child. Ask him to listen carefully and point to the picture that you say, or put a counter on it, or hold it up. Break the word into syllables leaving a pause between the syllables, eg '**cir – cle**'.

- Choose at least five pictures. Make sure the child has the same pictures that you have. Place a barrier between you and the child so that you cannot see each other's pictures. Say at least two words for the child, breaking the words into syllables, eg '**cir – cle**, **sci – ssors**'. The child listens, and arranges his pictures on his side of the barrier in the order he hears them. Ask the child what pictures he has so that he has to name them for you. Then remove the barrier to see if they match your pictures.

What did I say? (Listening and speaking activity)

Aim

To say longer words that contain the speech sound **s**: **sandal**, **sardine**, **soldier**, **surgeon**, **princess**, **seagull**, **minus**, **seven**, **delicious**, **police**, **Santa**, **dangerous**, **surfboard**, **sunny**, **salad**, **city**, **seaweed**, **salt**, **cinema**, **sausage**, **saddle**, **sofa**, **cereal**, **sandwich**, **furious**, **waitress**, **saucepan**, **tennis**, **scissors**, **curious**, **sixteen**, **sixty**, **sailor**, **seventeen**, **seventy**, **circle**, **octopus**, **sauce**, **singer**, **necklace**.

How?

By giving the child opportunities to hear, and see, you say longer words that contain **s** and to practise saying the words.

Resources

- At least two sets of the small pictures of longer words that contain **s** (pp194–199).

Instructions

You are the speaker and the child is the listener in these activities.

1. Choose two pictures, eg **cinema** and **tennis**. Put them on the table in front of the child and name them for him: '**Cinema. Tennis.**' Tell the child to listen carefully and then you name one of the pictures placed in front of him, eg '**Cinema**'. Then say 'What did I say?' The child listens and points to, or holds up, or puts a counter on the picture of the word he heard you say.

2. When you think the child is ready to listen and remember more words, choose three pictures, eg **cinema**, **tennis** and **sunny**. Put them on the table in front of the child and name them for him: '**Cinema. Tennis. Sunny**'.

Tell the child to listen carefully and then name two of the pictures placed in front of him, eg '**Sunny. Cinema**'. Then say 'What did I say?' The child listens and points to, or holds up, or puts a counter on the words he heard you say. Increase the number of words to make the activity more challenging when you think the child is ready.

Note: See Section 3 for variations and tips for this activity.

Roll and say (Speaking activity)

Aim

To say longer words that contain the speech sound **s: sandal, sardine, soldier, surgeon, princess, seagull, minus, seven, delicious, police, Santa, dangerous, surfboard, sunny, salad, city, seaweed, salt, cinema, sausage, saddle, sofa, cereal, sandwich, furious, waitress, saucepan, tennis, scissors, curious, sixteen, sixty, sailor, seventeen, seventy, circle, octopus, sauce, singer, necklace.**

How?

By giving the child opportunities to hear, and see, you say longer words that contain **s** and to practise saying the words.

Resources

- A set of six small pictures (pp194–199) with shapes on the back, cut up and laminated (photocopy the sheet of shapes (p83) on to the back of the pictures so that they are double sided).

- A dice.

- Template for a dice with a different shape on each face (p30).

Instructions

1. Spread the pictures out in front of the child, face down so that you can see the shapes on the back.

2. Roll the dice with shapes on it. The shapes on the dice match the shapes on the pictures. Turn over the picture that has the same shape as the dice, eg circle, so that you can see what the picture is, eg **sardine**.

3. Roll the dice with numbers on it. You have to say the word on your picture, eg **sardine**, the number of times on the dice, eg 5. Make sure you have the first turn so that you can demonstrate the activity to the child.

Variations

- Make the game competitive: the winner is the first person to say all of the six pictures in the activity, ie to throw all of the shapes on the dice.

- Roll the dice with shapes on it and turn over the picture that has the same shape on it, eg heart. Take it in turns to see how many times you can say the word in a minute. Use a one-minute salt timer.

Don't laugh! (Speaking activity)

Aim

To say longer words that contain the speech sound **s: police, salad, salt, sandwich, sausage, sauce, sardine, cereal, Santa, soldier, sailor, surgeon, singer, princess, sandal, city, necklace, octopus, dangerous, furious, delicious, waitress, circle, saddle, tennis, cinema, scissors, seagull, seaweed, surfboard, saucepan, minus, sunny, sofa, curious. sixteen, sixty, seven, seventeen, seventy.**

How?

By giving the child opportunities to hear, and see, you say longer words that contain **s** and to practise saying the words.

Resources

- Small pictures of longer words that contain **s** (pp194–199).
- Questions (p171).

Instructions

1. Ask the child to choose a word, the sillier the better! For example: **sausages** or **sardines**.

2. Then ask the child questions from page 171. (These are examples. You know the child and you know what will make him laugh, so make up your own questions to use with the ones here or instead of them.) He can answer your questions only with the word he has chosen, eg 'sausages'. The aim of the game is to answer the most questions without laughing. If you laugh, then your go is over.

Tip

Play this game in a group or whole-class setting. Have a group or class competition to see who can answer the most questions without laughing.

Questions

What's your name?	What would you say to the Queen if she came to tea?
Where do you live?	What is in your bag?
What do you clean your teeth with?	What is in your pockets?
What do you wash with?	What is your favourite ice cream?
What do you brush your hair with?	What do you write with?
What does your best friend look like?	What are you going to give to your mum for Christmas?
What do you want for your birthday?	Who do you like to dance with?
What do you like wearing?	What do you play football with?
What do you clean the house with?	What are you sitting on?
If you won a million pounds, what would you buy?	What are you wearing?

My progress

Date	I can ...	☺/☹	I need to work on ...
	Listen carefully and hear **s** in long words, eg **city**, **cinema**, **tennis**, without any help.		
	Listen carefully and hear **s** in long words, eg **city**, **cinema**, **tennis**, with help.		
	Say **s** in long words, eg **city**, **cinema**, **tennis**, without any help.		
	Say **s** in long words, eg **city**, **cinema**, **tennis**, with help.		

What's the next step?

- I can listen carefully and hear **s** in long words, eg **city**, **cinema**, **tennis**, without any help. **Start working on the words in Section 7. Continue playing listening games from the list of games in Section 9.**

- I can listen carefully and hear **s** in long words, eg **city**, **cinema**, **tennis**, with help. **Continue doing listening activities from Section 6. Do listening activities from earlier sections to review work you have done with the child. Play listening games from the list of games in Section 9. When the child can hear s in long words at least 70 per cent of the time in listening activities, start working on words in Section 7.**

- I can say **s** in long words, eg **city**, **cinema**, **tennis**, without any help. **Start working on words in Section 7. Continue playing speaking games from the list of games in Section 9.**

- I can say **s** in long words, eg **city**, **cinema**, **tennis**, with some help. **Continue working on speaking activities from Section 6. Do speaking activities from earlier sections to review work you have done with the child. Play speaking games from the list of games in Section 9. When the child can say s in long words at least 70 per cent of the time in activities, start working on words in Section 7.**

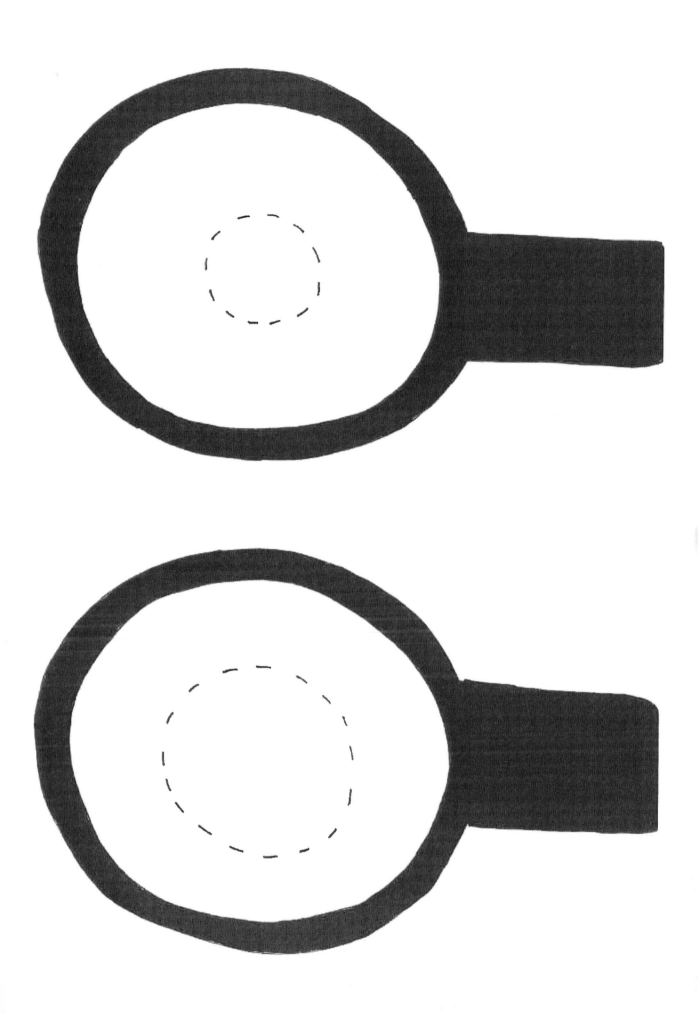

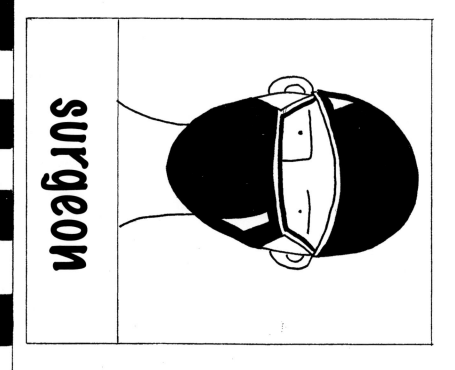

surgeon

princess

Look!

Look!

70 seventy

17 seventeen

sauce

sugar

Look!

Look!

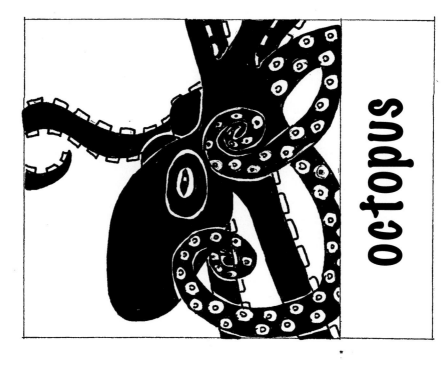

octopus

necklace

salt

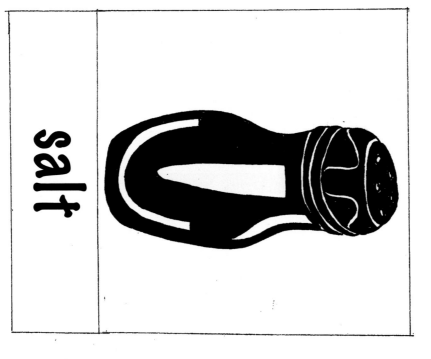

salad

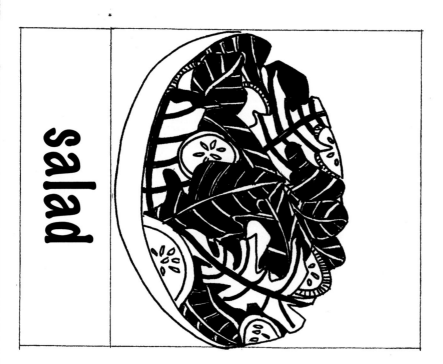

Look!

Look!

sunny

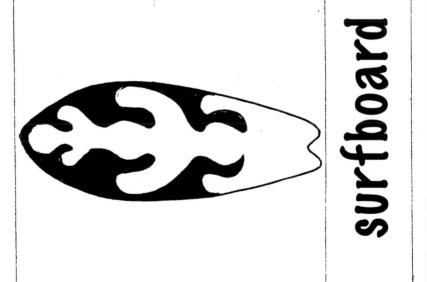

surfboard

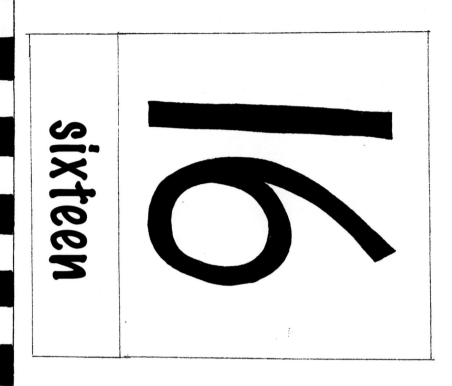

16

sixteen

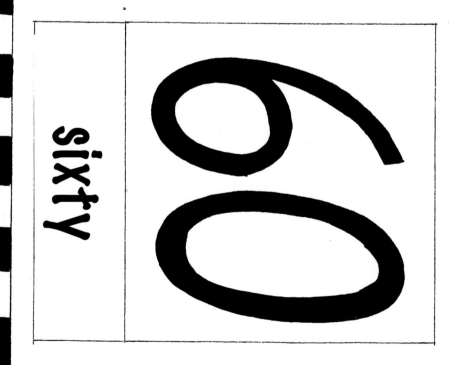

60

sixty

Look!

Look!

scissors

tennis

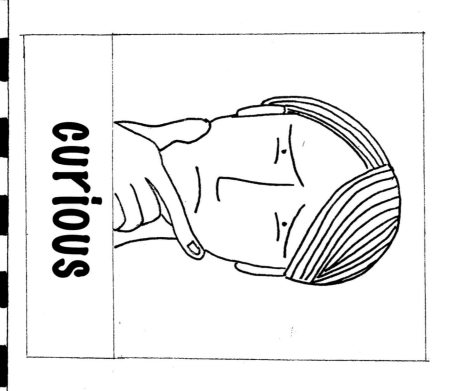

curious

saucepan

Look!

Look!

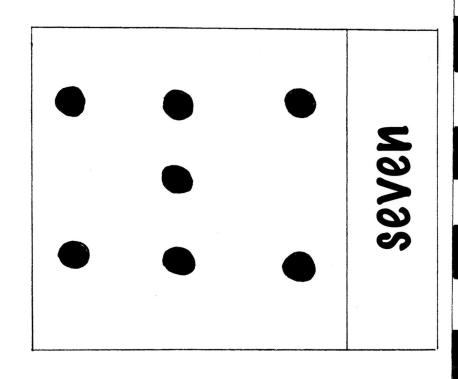

seven

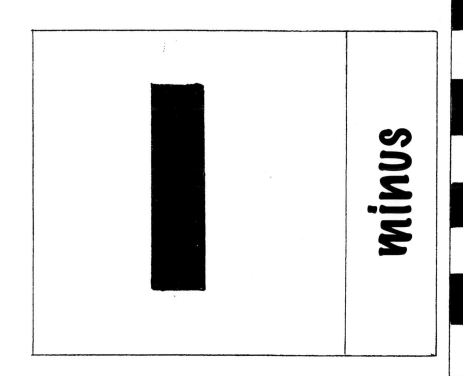

minus

look!

police

santa

Look!

dangerous

delicious

Look!

Mr.

Mrs.

Look!

waitress

furious

seagull

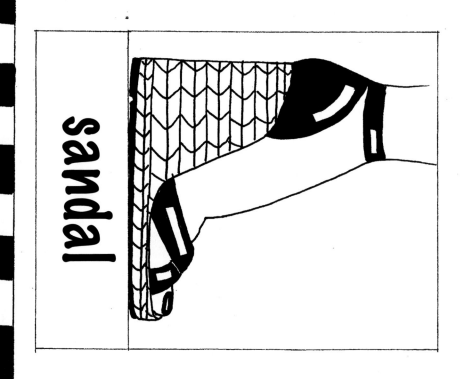

sandal

Look!

Look!

seaweed

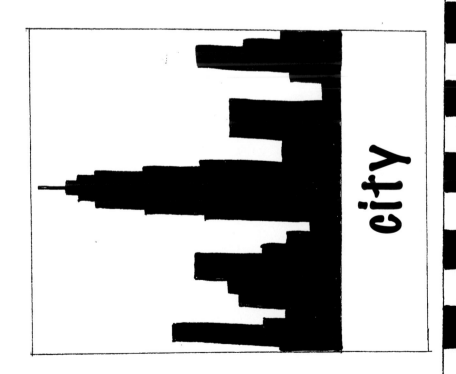

city

Look!

sofa

cinema

The End

Look!

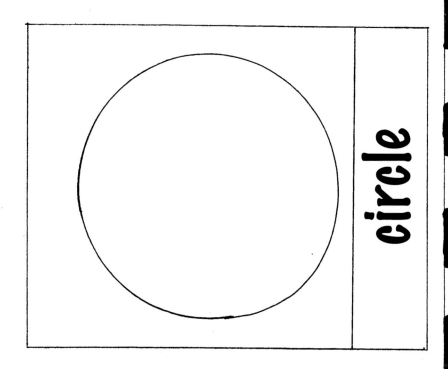

circle

sailor

saddle

sausage

Look!

Look!

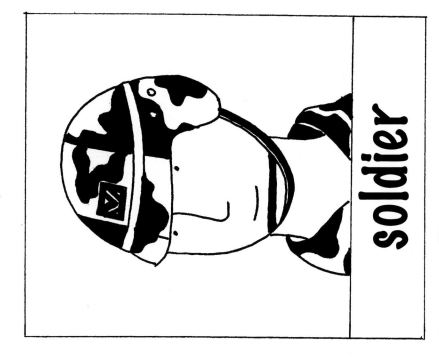

soldier

sardine

16 sixteen

17 seventeen

60 sixty

70 seventy

circle

sailor

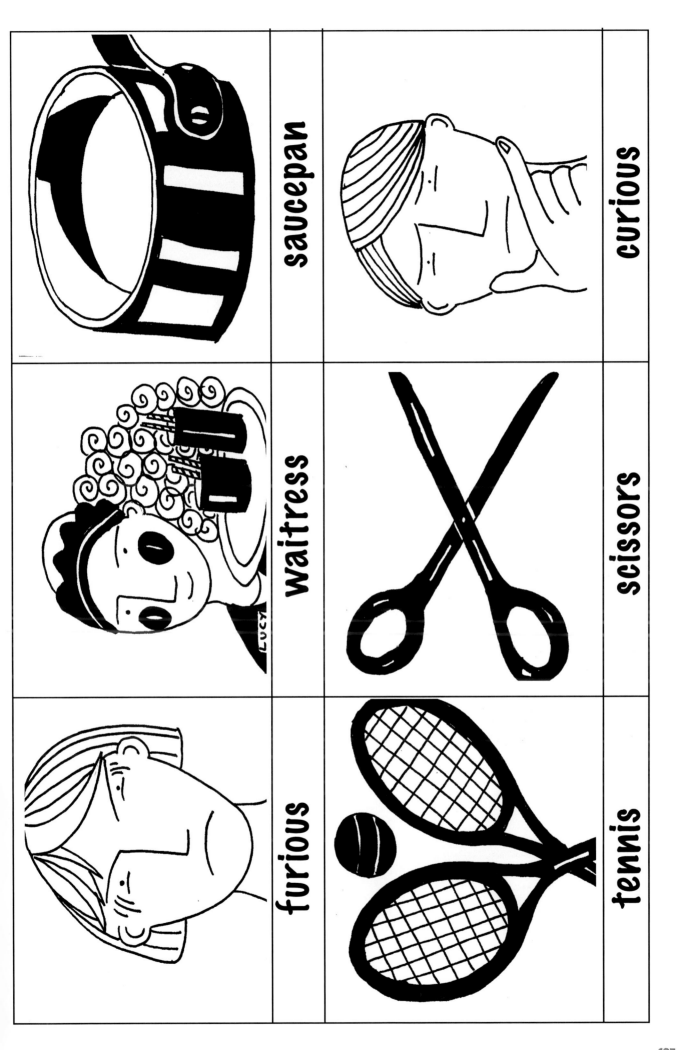

saucepan

curious

waitress

scissors

furious

tennis

surfboard

city

sunny

seaweed

salad

salt

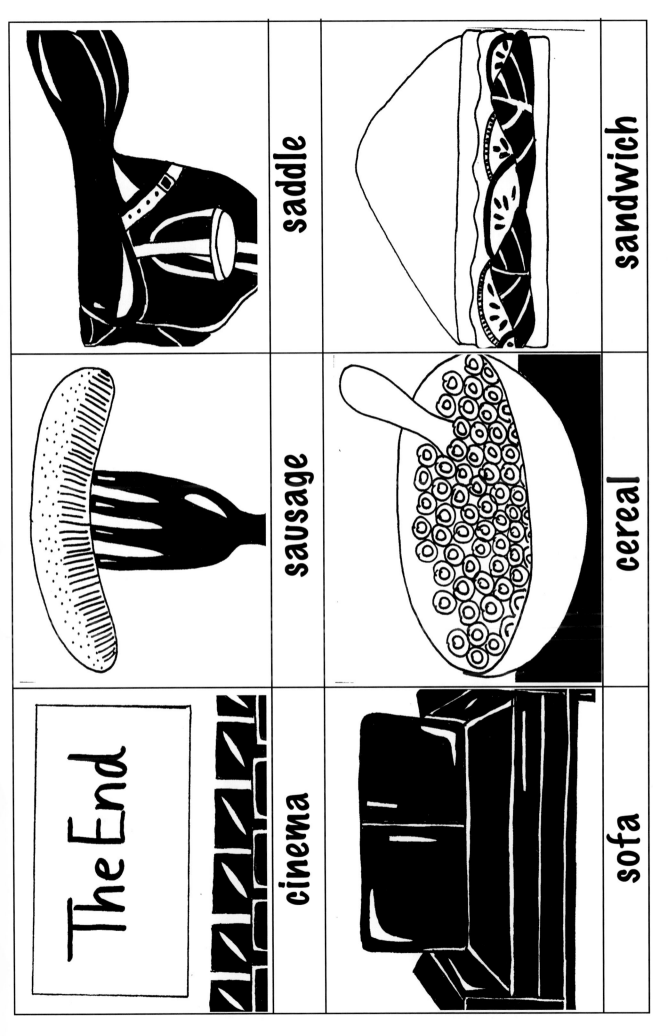

saddle

sandwich

sausage

cereal

The End

cinema

sofa

police

minus

santa

seven

dangerous

delicious

singer

Mr.

sauce

Mrs.

octopus

necklace

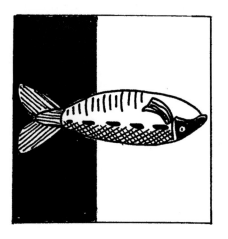

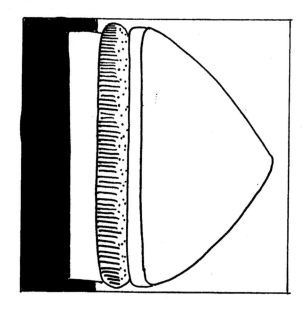

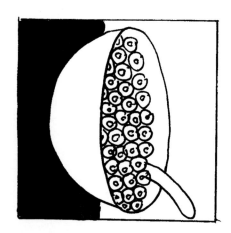

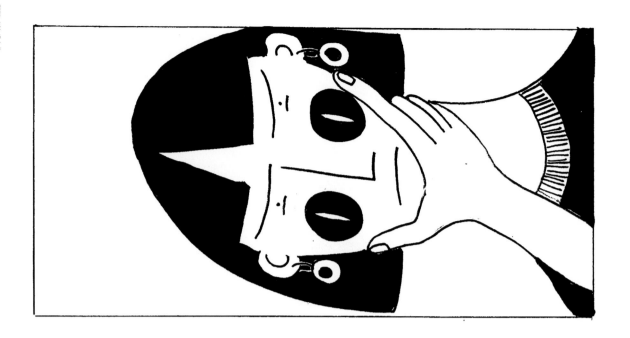

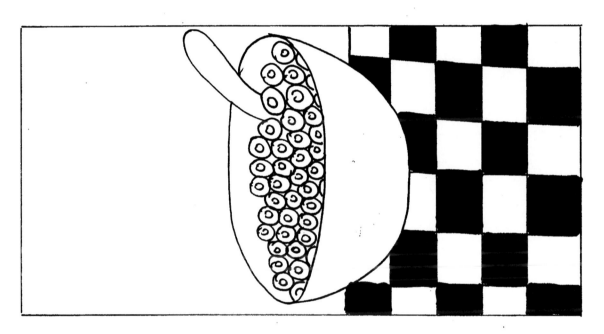

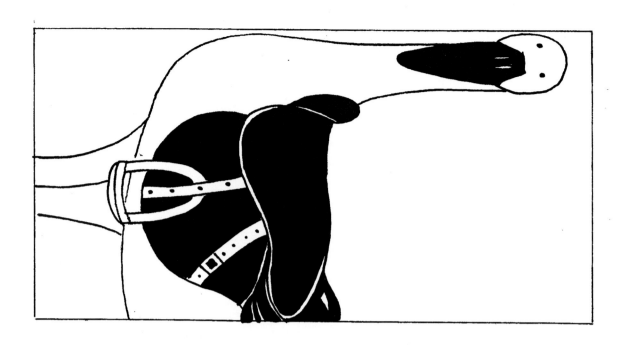

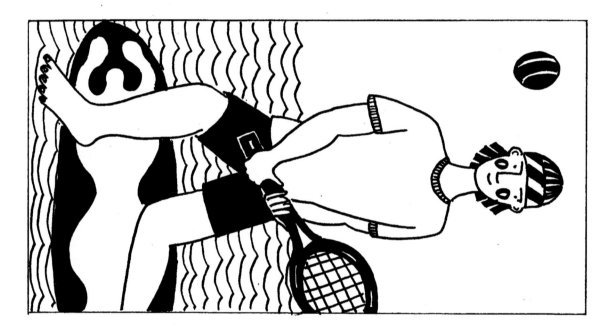

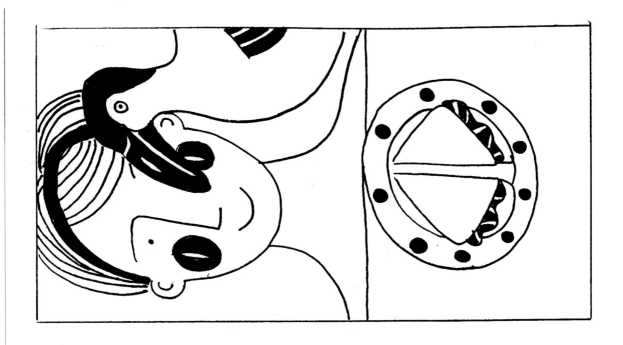

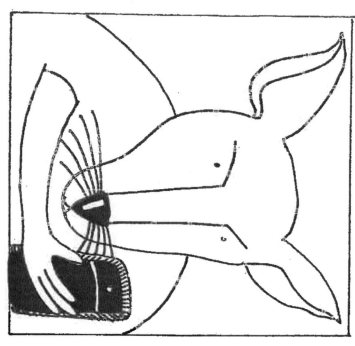

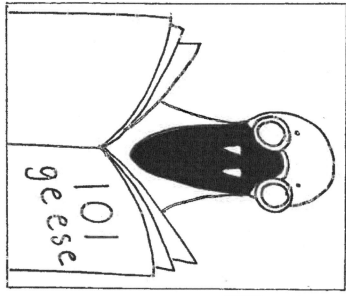

101
geese

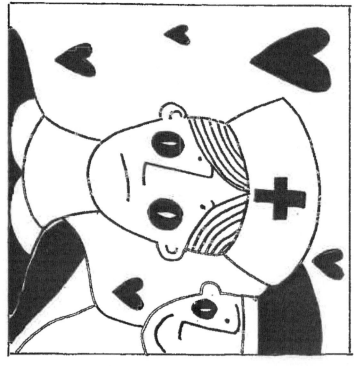

Jingles with s in long words

See advice at the end of Section 3 (p84–85) on how to use the jingles.

Jingle 1 (pictures on p200)

Listen

Can I have a sausage sandwich, please?

Certainly. Would you like a sardine in your sandwich?

No thank you. Just a sausage, please!

What about some seaweed?

No, thank you. Just a sausage, please!

Would you like some soy sauce?

No, thank you. Just a sausage, please!

What about some cereal in your sandwich?

Say the word

Can I have a sausage _____ (sandwich), please?

Certainly. Would you like a _____ (sardine) in your sandwich?

No thank you. Just a _____ (sausage), please!

What about some _____ (seaweed)?

No, thank you. Just a _____ (sausage), please!

Would you like some soy _____ (sauce)?

No, thank you. Just a _____ (sausage), please!

What about some ____ (cereal) in your sandwich?

Jingle 2 (pictures on p201)

Listen

The princess is furious

Oh dear! Why?

The princess is furious because someone stole her cereal

Oh dear!

The princess's sister, Sally, is curious

Curious about what?

Curious about who stole the princess's cereal

Does she know who stole the cereal?

No

Do you know who stole the princess's cereal?

Yes. Me! It was yummy!

Say the word

The princess is _____ (furious)

Oh dear! Why?

The princess is furious because someone stole her _____ (cereal)

Oh dear!

The princess's sister, Sally, is _____ (curious)

Curious about what?

Curious about who stole the princess's _____ (cereal)

Does she know who stole the _____ (cereal)?

No

Do you know who stole the _____ (princess's) cereal?

Yes. Me! It was yummy!

Jingle 3   (pictures on p202)

Listen

Can you put a saddle on a goose?

No, of course you can't!

But you could put a saddle on a horse

Can you play tennis on a surfboard?

No, of course you can't!

But you could play tennis on a tennis court

Can you make a sandwich with an octopus?

No, of course you can't!

But you could make a sandwich with my sister

Say the word

Can you put a saddle on a _____ (goose)?

No, of _____ (course) you can't!

But you could put a saddle on a _____ (horse)

Can you play _____ (tennis) on a surfboard?

No, of _____ (course) you can't!

But you could play tennis on a _____ (tennis) court

Can you make a sandwich with an _____ (octopus)?

No, of _____ (course) you can't!

But you could make a sandwich with my _____ (sister)

Jingle 4   (pictures on p203)

Listen

Yesterday, I saw an octopus in the cinema

Are you being serious or silly?

Silly

Yesterday, I sat on the sofa with Santa

Are you being serious or silly?

Silly

Yesterday, I made a delicious sandwich with a seagull

Are you being serious or silly?

Serious

Say the word

Yesterday, I saw an octopus in the _____ (cinema)

Are you being serious or _____ (silly)?

Silly

Yesterday, I sat on the sofa with _____ (Santa)

Are you being serious or _____ (silly)?

Silly

Yesterday, I made a delicious sandwich with a _____ (seagull)

Are you being serious or _____ (silly)?

Serious

Jingle 5 (pictures on p204)

Listen

I had a message from a mouse!

You had a massage from a moose?

No!

I had a lesson with a goose!

You had a lettuce and a juice?

No!

I saw a sailor chase a nurse!

You saw Santa choose a purse?

AHHHHHH!

Say the word

I had a _____ (message) from a mouse!

You had a _____ (massage) from a moose?

No!

I had a _____ (lesson) with a goose!

You had a _____ (lettuce) and a juice?

No!

I saw a _____ (sailor) chase a nurse!

You saw _____ (Santa) choose a purse?

AHHHHHH!

SECTION 7

SAYING S IN THE MIDDLE OF WORDS

Section 7: Saying s in the middle of words

Aim
To say the speech sound s in the middle of words: **parcel, message, person, dinosaur, muscle, icing, lesson, answer, messy, bicycle, classroom, pasta, bracelet, biscuit, question, icicle, castle, listen, Mr, Mrs**.

How?
By giving the child opportunities to hear, and see, you say words that end with **s** and to practise saying the words.

Resources
* A set of the large pictures (pp215–223) and a set of the small pictures (pp224–226) of words with **s** in the middle.

* Listening and speaking activities from Sections 3, 4, 5 and 6.

Instructions
Use the pictures in this section to play games and activities in Sections 3, 4, 5 and 6.

My progress

Date	I can ...	☺/☹	I need to work on ...
	Listen carefully and hear **s** in the middle of words, eg **biscuit, messy, pasta**, without any help.		
	Listen carefully and hear **s** in the middle of words, eg **biscuit, messy, pasta**, with some help.		
	Say **s** in the middle of words, eg **biscuit, messy, pasta**, without any help.		
	Say **s** in the middle of words, eg **biscuit, messy, pasta**, with some help.		

What's the next step?

- I can listen carefully and hear **s** in the middle of words, eg **biscuit**, **messy**, **pasta**, without any help. **Start working on Section 8. Continue playing listening games from the list of games in Section 9.**

- I can listen carefully and hear **s** in the middle of words, eg **biscuit**, **messy**, **pasta**, with help. **Continue doing listening activities from Section 7. Do listening activities from earlier sections to review work you have done with the child. Play listening games from the list of games in Section 9. When the child can hear s in the middle of words at least 70 per cent of the time in listening activities, start working on Section 8.**

- I can say **s** in the middle of words, eg **biscuit**, **messy**, **pasta**, without any help. **Start working on Section 8. Continue playing speaking games from the list of games in Section 9.**

- I can say **s** in the middle of words, eg **biscuit**, **messy**, **pasta**, with some help. **Continue doing speaking activities from Section 7. Do speaking activities from earlier sections to review work you have done with the child. Play speaking games from the list of games in Section 9. When the child can say s in the middle of words at least 70 per cent of the time in activities, start working on Section 8.**

Look!

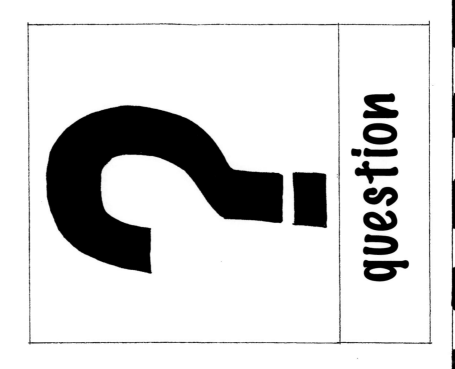

question

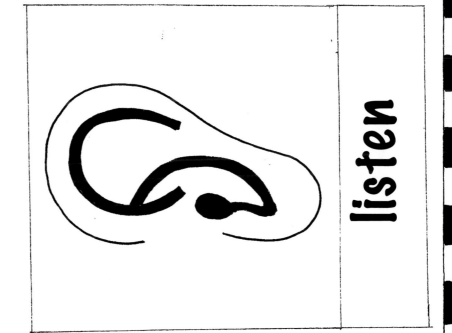

listen

215

Look!

biscuit

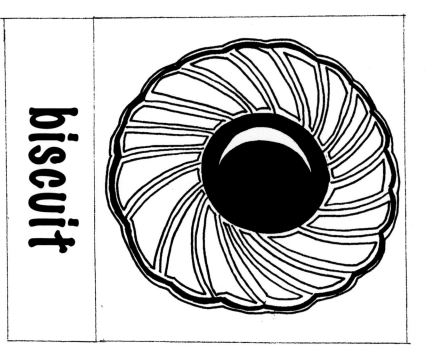

bracelet

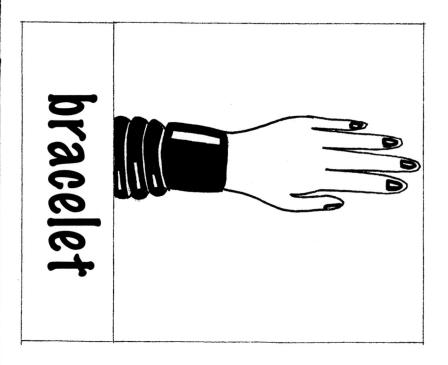

Look!

castle

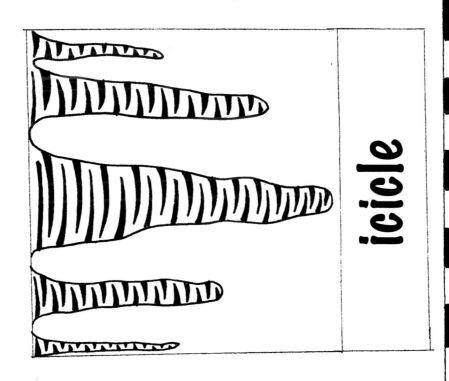

icicle

217

Look!

lesson

maths
1 + 1 = 2
2 + 2 = 4
3 + 3 = 6

answer

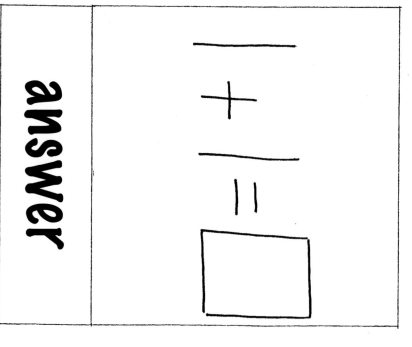

1 + 1 = ☐

Look!

classroom

bicycle

look!

messy

pasta

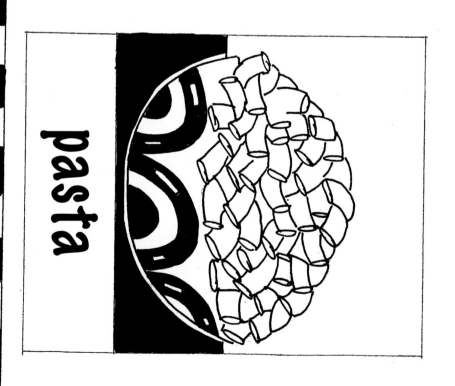

Look!

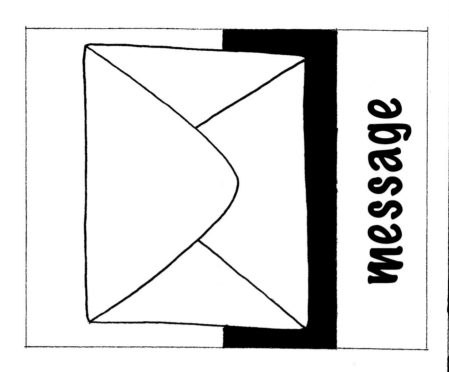

message

parcel

221

icing

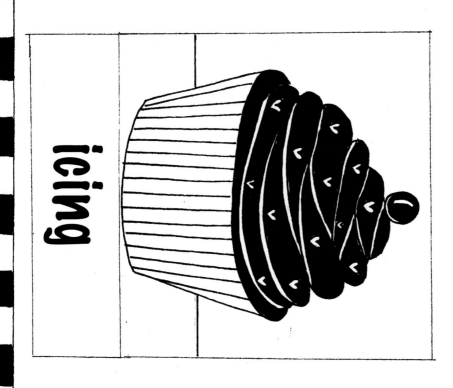

muscle

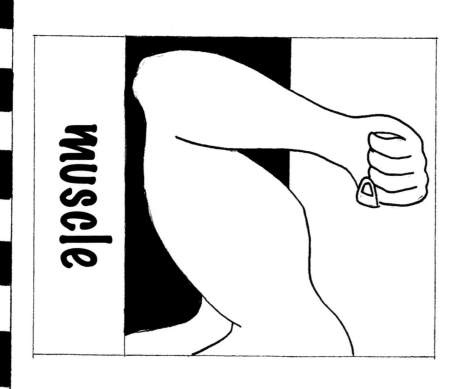

look!

Look!

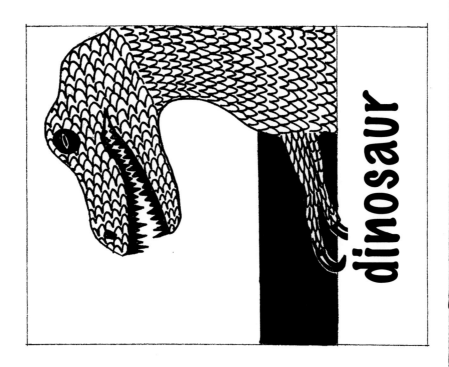

dinosaur

person

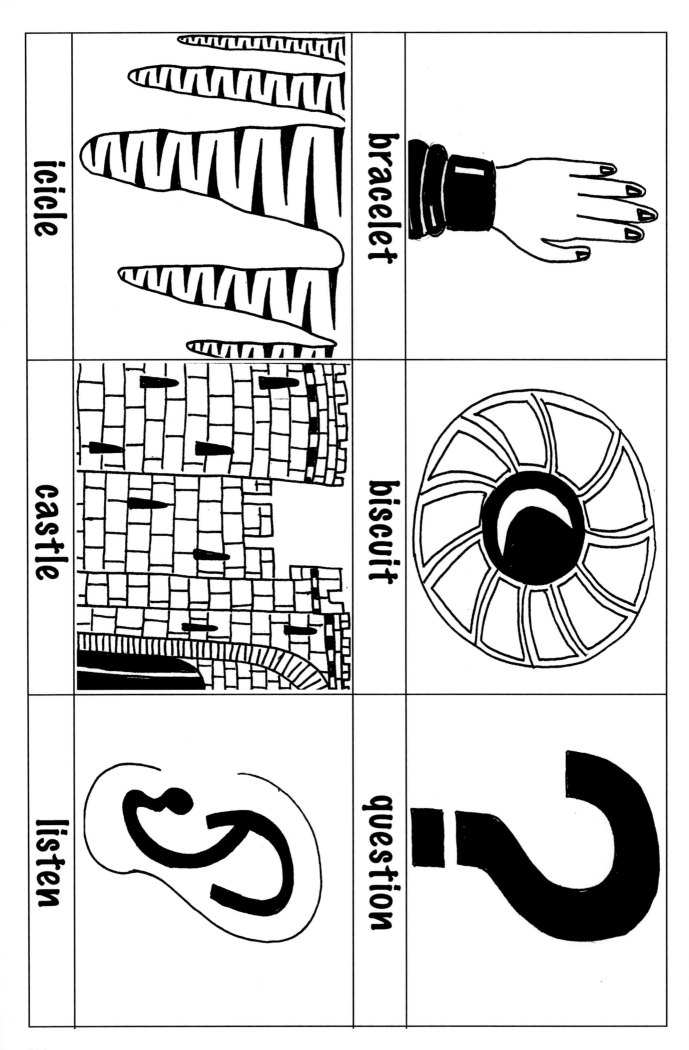

icicle

bracelet

castle

biscuit

listen

question

messy

pasta

answer

$1 + | = \square$

classroom

maths
$1 + 1 = 2$
$2 + 2 = 4$
$3 + 3 = 6$

lesson

$3 + 2 = 5$
$3 + 3 = 6$
$3 + 4 = 7$

bicycle

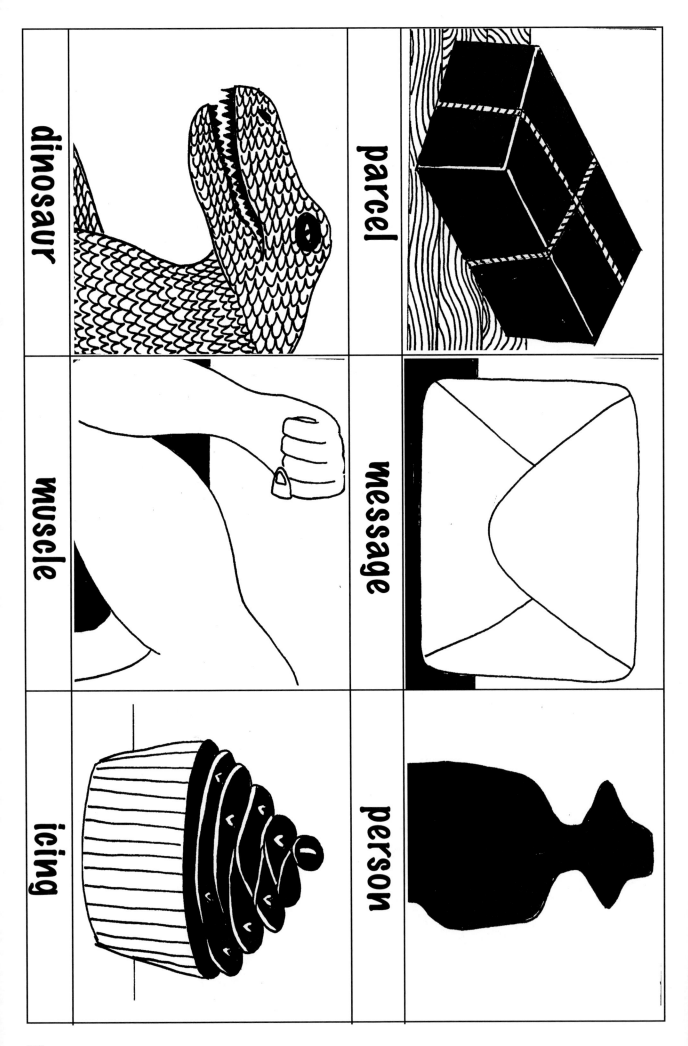

dinosaur

parcel

muscle

message

icing

person

SECTION 8

SAYING S IN PHRASES AND SENTENCES

Section 8: Saying s in phrases and sentences

General advice

- Choose which words you want to use in games. For example, you could start playing these games with short words that begin with s in Section 3, then use longer words in Section 4, then words in Section 5, and so on until you have progressed to working with words in Section 7.

- Try working with the same words until the child can say the words correctly in the games and activities most of the time, eg 70 per cent of the time. Then add some more words or change the set you are working on.

- Try rotating sets of words. For example, have three sets of ten words. Work on one set of ten words for a week and then work on a different set of ten words for another week, and another set of ten words for the third week. When you have completed this three-week cycle, go back to the original set of ten words and repeat.

Tell a story (Listening and speaking activity)

Aim
To say the words that contain **s** in this book in phrases and sentences in games and activities.

How?
By giving the child opportunities to hear, and see, you say words in phrases and sentences and to practise the words.

Resources
- At least five small pictures (pp117–118), eg **sock**, **sun**, **seat**, **soup**.

- Computer or pen and paper to write the story, or a tape recorder or video recorder to record the child telling the story.

Instructions
1. Put the pictures face down in a pile in front of the child.

2. Turn over the first picture and make up the beginning of a story using the word, eg **sock**. 'Once upon a time there was an octopus who had very cold tentacles! His feet got so cold that his mother knitted him a sock for each tentacle!'

3. Take it in turns to take a picture and make up the next part of the story using the word on the picture, eg **soup**. 'The octopus loved the socks and they did help, but he still felt cold. So his mother made him some hot soup.' Put the pictures face up on the table in a line as you use them in the story.

4. When you have finished the story, use the pictures to help the child remember and retell the story. Write the story on a computer or on paper or record it.

Tips

- Read the stories with feeling! Use different voices – a quiet voice, a slow voice, a deep voice, and so on, depending on the characters in your stories!

- Act your stories out!

Make up sentences (1) (Listening and speaking activity)

Aim

To say the words that contain **s** in this book in phrases and sentences in games and activities.

How?

By giving the child opportunities to hear, and see, you say words in phrases and sentences and to practise the words.

Resources

- At least six small pictures (pp152–154), eg **bus, face, mouse, dance, dress, goose**.

- Paper and crayons, felt-tip pens or coloured pencils.

Instructions

1. Put the pictures face down in a pile in front of the child.

2. Take it in turns to take a picture, eg **bus**, and use the word in a phrase, eg 'a big red **bus**', or in a sentence, eg 'I missed the **bus** this morning!'

3. Take it in turns to turn over two pictures, eg **bus** and **mouse**, and use both words in a phrase, eg 'a **mouse** on a **bus**', or a sentence, eg 'I saw a **mouse** sitting on a **bus**!'

4. Increase the number of pictures so that you increase the number of words that you have to use in a phrase or sentence, eg 'I saw a **mouse** in a dress talking to a **moose** and a **goose** sitting on a **bus**.' See who can make the longest sentence!

5. See how many the child can remember.

Variations

- Write the phrases or sentences and illustrate them. Cover up the writing so that the child can see the illustration only. See if she can remember the phrase or sentence.

- Choose at least four words and make up a short rhyme or poem using the words.

- Take it in turns to throw a dice to see how many words you have to use in a sentence, eg 5, and make a sentence containing that many words. For example: 'A **mouse** got a bus to see a **moose**, who had a **dance** with a **goose**, drinking a **juice**!'

- See how many words that start or end with **s** the child can use in a sentence in one minute. Use a one-minute salt timer.

Make a word web (Listening and speaking activity)

Aim

To say the words that contain **s** in this book in phrases and sentences in games and activities.

How?

By giving the child opportunities to hear, and see, you say words in phrases and sentences and to practise the words.

Resources

- At least four small pictures, eg **cinema**, **sandwich**, **seagull**, **soldier**.
- Paper, or a work book.
- Pencils, crayons or felt-tip pens.

Instructions

1. Let the child choose one of the small pictures. Draw a circle in the middle of the piece of paper and write the word in it, eg **cinema**. Ask the child to draw it so that you have a picture and the word.

2. Ask the child questions about the word. For example:
   Q: 'What is a cinema?'
   Possible answer: 'A place, a place where you watch films.'
   Q: 'Where do you find it?'
   A: 'In towns, in cities.'
   Q: 'What does it look like?'
   A: 'It is a big building with rooms where they show films. It's got big comfy seats. You can buy sweets and popcorn there.'

Q: 'What do you do in a cinema?'

A: 'You watch films.'

Q: 'Can you think of another place where you can watch films?'

A: 'You can watch films at home on the TV.'

Q: 'Do you like going to the cinema?'

3. Write the child's answers on the word web.

4. Keep the word webs in a work book or a word bag or folder. When you have at least three word webs, choose one. Make sure the child cannot see it. Tell the child about the word and ask her to guess what it is, eg 'It's a place. It's big. You go there to watch films. What is it?'

5. Reverse this activity with older children so that they choose a picture and give you clues to guess what it is.

Board game variation (Listening and speaking activity)

Aim

To say the words that contain **s** in this book in phrases and sentences in games and activities.

How?

By giving the child opportunities to hear, and see, you say words in phrases and sentences and to practise the words.

Resources

• A board game, eg snakes and ladders.

• A photocopy of the adjectives, eg *big, hot, expensive, shiny* (pp239–241), cut into cards.

• At least six small pictures of words you have been working on.

• A photocopy of the emotions (p31), eg *say it in a happy voice, say it in a sad voice, say it in an angry voice*, cut into cards.

Instructions

1. Set up the board game. Put the adjectives and the small pictures face down in two piles.

2. Take it in turns to take a picture from each pile before you have your go, eg *big*, **seagull**.

3. Make a sentence using the two words, eg 'I saw a *big* **seagull** on the beach.' Then have your go.

Variations

- A set of the emotion cards, eg **happy**, **sad**, **angry**. Set up a board game and put a pile of the emotion cards and a pile of the small pictures face down. Before each go, players take an emotion card, eg *say it in an angry voice*, and a small picture, eg **princess**, and say the word in the manner of the adjective.

- Put a pile of the emotion cards and a pile of the small pictures face down. Take it in turns to take a card from each pile, eg *say it in a tired voice*, and **police**, and say the word in the manner of the emotion. The other player has to guess what the emotion is.

- Put a pile of the emotion cards and a pile of the small pictures face down. Take it in turns to take a card from each pile, eg *say it in a sad voice* and **soldier**. Make a phrase or sentence using the word, eg 'See a **soldier**', and say it in the manner of the. The other player has to guess what emotion is on the card.

Continue the sentence (Listening and speaking activity)

Aim
To say the words that contain **s** in this book in phrases and sentences in games and activities.

How?
By giving the child opportunities to hear, and see, you say words in phrases and sentences and to practise the words.

Resources
- At least four small pictures, eg **sofa**, **salad**, **sausage**, **seagull**.

Instructions
1. Put the pictures face down in a pile.

2. You start by saying 'I went to the market and I bought a ...' and taking a picture from the pile, eg **sofa**.

3. The child says 'I went to the market and I bought a **sofa** and a ...' and takes a picture from the pile, eg **sausage**.

4. Keep going until a player cannot remember all the items they bought.

Variations
- Leave the pictures face up to help players remember what they bought.

- Change the place, eg I went to Jamaica and I saw ...; I went to the moon and I took ...I went to stay with the Queen and I took ...'.

Say the missing word (Listening and speaking activity)

Aim

To say the words that contain **s** in this book in phrases and sentences in games and activities.

How?

By giving the child opportunities to hear, and see, you say words in phrases and sentences and to practise the words.

Resources

- At least one of the jingles that uses the words you have been working on, eg:
  - Bee by bice
  - Roll a dice
  - Catch a bus
  - Fry some rice

Instructions

1. Read the jingle to the child at the end of a few sessions so that she knows it well.

2. Read the jingle, but leave out a word that contains the speech sound **s** in some lines (the number of words you leave out will depend on the level of the child). See if the child can remember the word and complete the sentence.

3. Gradually leave out more words in the rhyme and see if the child can remember them, eg:
   Bee by bice
   Roll a _____ (dice)
   Catch a _____ (bus)

Variations

- If the child cannot remember the words you have omitted from the jingles, sound them out, eg **d – ice** (**dice**). The child listens, puts the speech sounds together to make the word and says it: **dice**.

- Older children might be able to read some of the jingles with you.

Think of a word (Speaking activity)

Aim
To say the words that contain **s** in this book in phrases and sentences in games and activities.

How?
By giving the child opportunities to hear, and see, you say words in phrases and sentences and to practise the words.

Resources
- Photocopy of the grid template *Can you think of …?* (p242).
- Pencils or pens.

Instructions
1. Read the first question with the child: *Can you think of an animal that begins with the sound **s**?*

2. The child has to think of a word that begins with the sound **s**, eg **seal**, **seagull**. There is space to write his answer, if you want to record it. Ask the second question: *Can you think of a colour that begins with the sound **s**?* Let the child look at the small pictures to help him think of answers if he needs support.

3. See if you can answer all the questions and add one of your own!

Variation
- Make the activity into a competition. Players write their answers and don't show each other what they have written until the end.

Would you rather …? (Listening and speaking activity)

Aim
To say the words that contain **s** in this book in phrases and sentences in games and activities.

How?
By giving the child opportunities to hear, and see, you say words in phrases and sentences and to practise the words.

Resources
The *Would you rather …?* sheet (p243), cut up into pieces and laminated.

235

Instructions

1. Put the cards in a pile face down and take the first card from the pile. Read it out loud, eg *Would you rather eat soap or wash with soup?*

2. When the child answers the question, eg 'A goose on a horse', ask her 'Why?'

3. When the child has answered the questions, take another card.

4. Take it in turns to answer the *Would you rather ...?* questions.

Variations

- Make your own *Would you rather ...?* questions using words with **s** that you have worked on in this book.

- Older children might be able to read some of the *Would you rather ...?* questions.

- Carry out a survey with older children, eg ask teachers and children at least four of the *Would you rather ...?* questions and present the results.

I like / don't like (Listening and speaking activity)

Aim

To say the words that contain **s** in this book in phrases and sentences in games and activities.

How?

By giving the child opportunities to hear, and see, you say words in phrases and sentences and to practise the words.

Resources

The *I like / I don't like* resource (p244), photocopied, laminated and cut into cards.

Instructions

1. Put the cards face down in a pile and take the first card from the pile. Read it out loud, eg *going to the cinema*.

2. Put the card on the 'I like' square or on the 'I don't like' square, depending on whether you like going to the cinema or not. For example: 'I like going to the cinema'.

3. Tell the child one thing about going to the cinema, eg 'I went to the cinema last week and saw a sad film.'

4. Take it in turns to take a card, tell each other if you like it or not and tell each other one thing about it (see the cards for suggestions).

Variations

- Make your own versions using words with **s** that you have worked on in this book.

Make up sentences (2) (Speaking activity)

Aim

To say the words that contain **s** in this book in phrases and sentences in games and activities.

How?

By giving the child opportunities to hear, and see, you say words in phrases and sentences and to practise the words.

Resources

Photocopies of the nouns (pp245–246), the verbs (pp247–248) and the adjectives (pp239–241), laminated and cut into cards.

Instructions

1. Put the three sets of cards in piles face down.

2. Take at least two noun cards, a verb card and an adjective card, eg nouns – Santa, a sailor; verb – sold; adjective – massive.

3. Make a sentence with your words. For example: 'Santa sold a massive sailor.' 'A massive sailor sold Santa.' 'Santa and a massive sailor sold his sleigh.'

Variations

- How long can you make your sentence? For example: 'One cold snowy day, Santa sold a massive sailor to the captain of a ship.'

- How many sentences can you make in a minute? Take at least four cards, make a sentence, take another four, make another sentence, and so on.

- Spread all the cards out so that you can see them. See who can make the silliest sentence. For example: 'A princess and a furious goose sailed across the sea on a salami sandwich.'

- Add one word each to make a sentence together. For example:
  A: A nurse
  B: saw
  A: a dangerous
  B: goose.

Happy families (Speaking and listening activity)

Aim

To say the words that contain **s** in this book in phrases and sentences in games and activities.

How?

By giving the child opportunities to hear, and see, you say words in phrases and sentences and to practise the words.

Resources

- Photocopies of the pages of families: **Mr Sew** the tailor and family; **Mr Send** the postman and family; **Mr Sing** the musician and family; **Mr Price** the shopkeeper and family; **Mr Seal** the zookeeper and family; **Mr Sum** the teacher and family; **Mr Siren** the policeman and family; **Mr Muscle** the weight trainer and family; **Mr Messy** the cleaner and family; **Mr Cement** the builder and family (pp249–258), laminated and cut up into cards.

Instructions

1. You need at least three players. Shuffle the cards and deal them out.

2. Players organise their hand into families. If they have all four members of a family, they put the family down on the table.

3. The aim is to collect as many families as you can. The winner is the person who has the most families.

4. Players ask each other for cards that they don't have. For example, if you have Mr Send the postman and his wife, you need Master and Miss Send to complete the family. When it is your go, you can choose a player and ask them if they have one of these, eg 'Have you got Miss Send, the postman's daughter?' If the player has the card that you have asked for, they must give it to you and you can have another go. If they do not have the card, the next person has their go.

Adjectives (1)

dirty	cold	hot
small	big	wet
hungry	short	long
red	round	thirsty
shiny	tall	heavy

Adjectives (2)

soggy	sad	massive
delicious	curious	furious
fabulous	fantastic	marvellous
similar	soft	dangerous
salty	same	safe

Adjectives (3)

silly	sensible	selfish	
silent	sick	serious	
tasty	soppy	simple	

Can you think of …

an animal that begins with the sound s?	
a colour that begins with the sound s?	
a food that begins with the sound s?	
a job that begins with the sound s?	
a country that begins with the sound s?	
a piece of clothing that begins with the sound s?	
a sport that begins with the sound s?	
a part of the body that begins with the sound s?	
a name that begins with the sound s?	

Would you rather ...

Would you rather go to the cinema and watch a film with a mouse or a horse? Why?	Would you rather eat a seaweed stew or sausage ice cream? Why?
Would you rather swim with an octopus or fly with a seagull? Why?	Would you rather sing to a seal or dance with a seagull? Why?
Would you rather eat soap or wash with soup? Why?	Would you rather kiss an octopus or kiss a moose? Why?
Would you rather walk to school with a goose or ride to school on a moose? Why	Would you rather be a famous singer or Santa? Why?
Would you rather eat rice with a sword or eat a sausage with a pair of scissors? Why?	Would you rather wear a dress made of seaweed or a dress made of sardines? Why?
Would you rather wear a suit and no socks or socks and no suit? Why?	Would you rather have a seagull or an octopus for a nurse? Why?
Would you rather live in a house made of ice or a house made of soap? Why?	Would you rather put a sausage on your cereal or put a sardine on your cereal? Why?

I like / I don't like

I like	I don't like

riding a horse + tell me one thing, eg how often you ride a horse	having cereal for breakfast + tell me one thing, eg your favourite cereal
washing with smelly soap + tell me one thing, eg your favourite smelly soap	going on a bus + tell me one thing, eg where you go by bus
chocolate mousse + tell me one thing, eg if you have ever made chocolate mousse	running a race + tell me one thing, eg if you are fast
riding a bicycle + tell me one thing, eg what colour your bike is	mice + tell me one thing, eg if you have seen a mouse in your house
singing + tell me one thing, eg what your favourite song is	going to the cinema + tell me one thing, eg what your favourite film is
making sandcastles + tell me one thing, eg if your sandcastle had a moat?	sewing + tell me one thing, eg what you have sewn
Santa + tell me one thing, eg if you have ever seen or heard his reindeer	doing sums + tell me one thing, eg if you like maths

Nouns

a seagull	a sardine	Santa
a goose	a prince	a princess
Sue	a nurse	a sailor
an octopus	a horse	Simon
a house	a moose	a mouse

Nouns

a castle	a biscuit	a sock
a salad	a sandwich	the sea
a song	a cinema	an ambulance
a hospital	medicine	a bus

Verbs

sent	sat	sold
sang	asked	said
swam	saw	sailed
sacked	persuaded	saved
seemed	searched	upset

Verbs

seized	selected	separated
sobbed	sorted	celebrated

Mr. Messy
The Cleaner

Mrs. Messy
The Cleaner's wife

Master Messy
The Cleaner's son

Miss Messy
The Cleaner's daughter

Mr. Price
The shopkeeper

Mrs. Price
The shopkeeper's wife

Master Price
The shopkeeper's son

Miss Price
The shopkeeper's daughter

Mr. Send
The postman

Mrs. Send
The postman's wife

Master Send
The postman's son

Miss Send
The postman's daughter

Mr. Sing
The musician

Mrs. Sing
The musician's wife

Master Sing
The musician's son

Miss Sing
The musician's daughter

Mr. Muscle
The weight trainer

Mrs. Muscle
The weight trainer's wife

Master Muscle
The weight trainer's son

Miss Muscle
The weight trainer's daughter

Mr. Sew
The tailor

Mrs. Sew
The tailor's wife

Master Sew
The tailor's son

Miss Sew
The tailor's daughter

Mr. Siren
The policeman

Mrs. Siren
The policeman's wife

Master Siren
The policeman's son

Miss Siren
The policeman's daughter

Mr. Sum
The teacher

Mrs. Sum
The teacher's wife

Master Sum
The teacher's son

Miss Sum
The teacher's daughter

Mr. Seal
The zoo keeper

Mrs. Siren
The zoo keeper's wife

Master Siren
The zoo keeper's son

Miss Siren
The zoo keeper's daughter

Mr. Cement
The builder

Mrs. Cement
The builder's wife

Master Cement
The builder's son

Miss Cement
The builder's daughter

SECTION 9

GAMES TO PLAY USING WORDS FROM ALL SECTIONS IN THE BOOK

Section 9: Games to play using words from all sections in the book

Contents

1. Pairs

2. Kim's game

3. Find the picture

4. Find the coin

5. Which picture?

6. Catch a picture

7. Bowling

8. Goal!

9. What is it?

10. Draw a picture!

11. Guess what?

12. Listen and colour

13. Listen and do

14. Charades

15. Make a sentence (noughts and crosses)

Game 1: Pairs (Speaking game)

What you need to play:

- At least two sets of small pictures of words you have been working on.

How to play

1. Shuffle the pictures and place them face down on the table.

2. Take it in turns to turn over two pictures.

3. Name each picture as you turn it over, eg '**Sun**. **Sock**'.

4. If the pictures are the same, eg **sock** and **sock**, you keep the pair. If they are different, eg **sun** and **sock**, you put them back on the table face down. The winner is the person who has the most pairs.

Game 2: Kim's game (Speaking game)

What you need to play

- At least one set of small pictures of words that you have been working on.

How to play

1. Put at least three pictures in front of the child.

2. Name the pictures and talk about them with the child to make the pictures more memorable, eg '**Sock**. My son wears Spiderman **socks**!' '**Seal**. **Seals** live in the sea. I saw one on holiday last year.'

3. Tell the child to look at the pictures and 'take a photo' in his mind (mime taking a picture with an imaginary camera) to help him remember them.

4. Ask the child to close his eyes.

5. Take away one of the pictures.

6. Ask the child to open his eyes and see if he can remember what the missing picture is.

Variation

- Make the game more challenging by increasing the number of pictures you use and the number of pictures you take away when the child closes his eyes.

Game 3: Find the picture (Listening and speaking game)

What you need to play

- A set of small pictures of words that you have been working on.

- Some Blu-Tack to stick the pictures around the room, eg on the door, on the back of a chair.

How to play

1. Show the child at least two pictures.

2. Name the pictures, eg 'Look! **Sow** and **sea**'. Talk about them a little to help the child remember the pictures.

3. Ask the child to close her eyes.

4. Hide the pictures and ask the child to open her eyes.

5. Ask her to find one of the pictures, eg 'Find **sea**'.

6. Reverse the game so that the child hides the pictures and tells you which one to find.

Variation

- Make the game more challenging by increasing the number of pictures you hide and the number of pictures you ask the child to find. For example, hide four pictures and ask the child to find two of them.

Game 4: Find the coin (Listening and speaking game)

What you need to play

- A set of at least six small pictures of words that you have been working on.
- A coin.

How to play

1. Put at least six of the small pictures in front of the child.

2. Name the pictures with the child, eg '**Horse. Moose. Mouse. Face. Bus. Dice.**'

3. Tell the child to close his eyes.

4. Hide a coin under one of the pictures.

5. Tell the child to open his eyes. The aim of the game is to find the coin. The child has to say which picture he thinks the coin is under, eg **bus**. Keep a record of how many guesses the child has before he finds the coin.

6. Reverse the game so that the child hides the coin and you guess which picture it is under. The winner is the person who finds the coin with the least number of guesses.

Variation

- Make the game more challenging by increasing the number of coins you hide. For example, hide three coins and the child has to guess which pictures they are under.

Game 5: Which picture? (Listening and speaking game)

What you need to play

- A set of small pictures of words you have been working on.

- Two cups (make sure you can't see through them).

- A coin or a counter or a small toy that will fit under the cups.

How to play

1. Choose two pictures and name them with the child, eg '**Sock**. **Seat**'.

2. Turn the cups upside down and place them at the top of the pictures.

3. Tell the child to close her eyes and put the coin, counter or small toy under one of the cups.

4. Ask the child to open her eyes. The aim of the game is for the child to guess which cup the coin, counter or small toy is under. The child names the picture that the cup is on, eg **sock**, and then looks under the cup to see if the item is underneath.

5. Reverse the game so that the child hides the item and you guess which cup it is under.

Game 6: Catch a picture (Listening and speaking game)

What you need to play

- A set of small pictures of words that you have been working on.

- Paper clips to attach to the pictures that you are using in the game.

- A fishing rod: make a fishing rod by attaching some string to a piece of wood or a pencil and tie a small magnet to the end of the string.

How to play

1. Put a paper clip on each of the small pictures that you are using in the game. Place the pictures face down on a flat surface or in a large bowl or similar container.

2. Take turns to 'catch a fish' with the rod and name the picture, eg **seagull**.

Variations

- See if you can catch a pair of pictures, eg **seagull** and **seagull**.

- Spread the pictures out picture side up and take it in turns to tell each other which picture to catch: eg 'Catch **circle**', 'Catch **sailor** and **Santa**!' Make this game more challenging by increasing the number of pictures you ask each other to catch.

Game 7: Bowling (Listening and speaking game)

What you need to play
- Two plastic bottles or skittles.

- A set of small pictures of words you have been working on.

- Blu-Tack to stick the pictures on to the bottles or skittles.

- A small ball.

How to play
1. Choose two pictures, eg **Sue** and **Si**.

2. Attach the pictures to bottles or skittles with Blu-Tack, eg put **Sue** on one skittle and put **Si** on the other skittle, or put a picture under each skittle.

3. To play this game as a listening game, give the ball to the child. Name one of the pictures on one of the skittles, eg **Sue**. The child listens and points to the picture that she heard you name. If she is right, she tries to knock the skittle over with the ball.

4. To play this game as a speaking game, let the child name one of the pictures, eg **saw**. You listen and point to the picture that you heard her name. If you are right, you roll the ball and try to knock over the skittle.

Game 8: Goal! (Listening and speaking game)

What you need to play
- A set of small pictures of words you have been working on.

- A bean bag or a small ball.

- Two boxes or containers, eg buckets.

- Blu-Tack to stick the pictures on to the boxes or containers.

How to play
1. Choose two pictures of words that you have been working on, eg **biscuit** and **bicycle**. Attach the pictures to the containers or place them in front of the containers.

2. To play this game as a listening game, give the bean bag or ball to the child. Name one of the pictures, eg **bicycle**. The child listens and points to the picture that he heard you name: **bicycle**. If he is right, he tries to throw the bean bag or ball into the appropriate container.

3. To play this game as a speaking game, let the child name one of the pictures, eg **biscuit**. You listen and point to the picture that you heard him name. If you are right, you throw the ball into the corresponding container.

Game 9: What is it? (Speaking game)

What you need to play
- At least one set of small pictures of words you have been working on.

- Plasticine or playdough.

How to play
1. Put the pictures face down in a pile in front of the players.

2. Take a picture from the pile. Do not show it to anyone else.

3. Take some playdough or plasticine and make a model of the picture.

4. The child has to guess what it is.

5. Take it in turns to take a picture and make a model of it for the other player to guess what it is.

Variations
- Limit the number of guesses to three!

- Give the child a minute to guess what your model is! Use a one-minute salt timer.

Game 10: Draw a picture! (Speaking game)

What you need to play
- At least one set of small pictures of words you have been working on.

- Paper and pencils or pens.

How to play

1. Put the pictures in a pile face down in front of the players.

2. Take a picture. Do not show it to anyone else.

3. Draw the picture.

4. Ask the child to guess what the picture is as you are drawing it.

5. Take it in turns to take a picture and draw it for the other player to guess what it is.

Variations

- Limit the number of guesses to six or fewer!

- Give the child a minute to guess what your picture is! Use a one-minute salt timer.

Game 11: Guess what? (Listening and speaking game)

What you need to play

- At least one set of small pictures of words you have been working on.

How to play

1. Choose a picture. Do not show it to anyone else.

2. Describe the picture for the child to guess what it is. For example: 'You wear them on your feet. You wear them in the summer, not in the winter' (sandals).

3. If this is too difficult for the child, put out at least three pictures and describe one of them. The child listens to your description and points to the picture.

4. Reverse the game where possible so that the child describes the picture and you guess what it is.

Variations

- Limit the number of clues you give the child to four, or fewer!

- Give the child a minute to guess what your picture is! Use a one-minute salt timer.

Game 12: Listen and colour (Listening and speaking game)

What you need to play

- Two identical sets of small pictures of words you have been working on, one for you and one for the child. Do not laminate them.

- A barrier that you can place between yourself and the child so that you cannot see each other's pictures.

How to play

1. With younger children, eg aged three to four, put at least two pictures in front of the child, eg **Santa** and **sausage**.

2. Ask the child to colour one of the pictures, eg 'Colour **Santa**'. To make the game more challenging increase the number of pictures and the number of colours. For example: 'Colour **Santa** red and the **sausage** purple', 'Colour **Santa's** legs blue and his nose orange.'

3. With children over four, make this game more challenging by placing a barrier between yourself and the child so that you cannot see each other's pictures. Put at least two pictures behind the barrier. Colour one of the pictures, or colour both of them using different colours. Then give instructions to the child, eg 'Colour the **camel** green and the **cooker** blue.' When the child has finished, remove the barrier to see if you have coloured the same pictures.

4. Reverse the game where possible so that the child gives you instructions.

Tip

Keep instructions short to make sure that the child can follow them. Children who are developing in a typical way can follow usually instructions as follows:

- Between the ages of 20 and 27 months, instructions containing two key words, eg Colour Santa's nose.

- Between the ages of 28 and 36 months, instructions containing three key words, eg Colour Santa's nose blue.

- Between the ages of 34 and 42 months, instructions containing four key words, eg Colour Santa's nose and hat blue (Knowles & Masidlover, 1982).

5. With children over four, make this game more challenging by placing a barrier between yourself and the child so that you cannot see each other's pictures. Put at least two pictures behind the barrier. Colour one of the pictures, or colour both of them using different colours. Then give instructions to the child, eg 'Colour **Santa** green and the **sausage** blue'. When the child has finished, remove the barrier to see if you have coloured the same pictures.

6. Reverse the game where possible so that the child gives you instructions.

Game 13: Listen and do (Listening and speaking game)

What you need to play

- Two identical sets of small pictures, one for you and one for the child.

- A selection of objects that are small enough to put on the pictures, eg a toy car, a button, a teaspoon, a toy animal, a small teddy. You need two of each so that you and the child have the same objects.

- A barrier that you can place between yourself and the child so that you cannot see each other's pictures.

How to play

1. Choose at least two pictures, eg **sun** and **safe**, and two objects, eg a toy pig and a button. Put the objects on the pictures on your side of the barrier so that the child cannot see them. For example, put the pig on the picture of the **sun** and the button on the picture of the **safe**.

2. Ask the child to do the same: 'Put the pig on the **sun** and the button on the **safe**.'

3. When he has finished, raise the barrier to see if he has the same pictures and objects as you.

4. Reverse the game so that the child gives the instructions and you listen and do.

Game 14: Charades (Speaking game)

What you need to play

- A set of actions to perform (p. 271), eg Have a sword fight!

How to play

1. Put the cards in a pile face down.

2. Take it in turns to pick up a card and mime what it says.

3. The winner is the person who guesses the most mimes correctly.

Variations

- Make up mimes with the child using the words you have been working on.

Game 15: Make a sentence (noughts and crosses) (Speaking game)

What you need to play

- Pens or pencils and paper.

- At least nine words containing **s**.

How to play

1. Draw a grid with nine boxes. Write one word in each box as in the example below.

bus	city	face
salt	cereal	seagull
sandwich	sock	tennis

2. Take it in turns to choose a box. To put your nought or cross in the box, you have to make a sentence containing the word in the box. For example: I play tennis every weekend.

3. The winner is the person who gets a horizontal, vertical or diagonal line of noughts or crosses.

Charades

Chase a seagull!	Ride a horse!
Wash your face!	Put a saddle on a horse!
Go on a surfboard!	Win a race!
Pack a case!	Have a sword fight!
Ride a bicycle!	Sip a hot drink!
Roll a dice!	Smell a smelly sock!
Saw some wood!	Watch a film in the cinema!
Play tennis!	Sing a song!
Give a fish to a seal!	Put on a necklace!
Look for a mouse!	Ride with Santa in his sleigh!

SECTION 10
SESSION PLANS

Section 10: **Session plans**

These session plans are for a child aged three and a half to seven years old, who is not saying **s** in words in his talking. He may say **t** instead of **s**, for example tea instead of sea, tore instead of saw; or he may say **d** instead of **s**, for example door instead of saw.

Aim
To help him say **s** in his talking.

How?
- By showing him how his mouth works, eg tongue movements, lip movements.

- By helping him to hear the speech sound **s** and to hear the speech sound **s** in words. The child may think he is saying **s**, so he thinks others can understand what he wants to tell them. You need to help him realise that he is not saying **s**, which can make it hard for others to understand what he wants to say.

- By helping him to make the speech sound **s** and then say **s** in words, eg **sea**, **seat**, **sock**, **sandwich**.

1. To help the child to say the speech sound s – Section 1 and Section 2.

What?	Why?	How?	Next step?
Mouth exercises	To help the child learn about his mouth and movements we make for speech.	**Section 1:** 1. Look in a mirror, eg 'Show me your tongue. Show me your teeth.' 2. Do single movements together with a mirror, eg 'Can you put your tongue up to your nose?'	**This is easy:** Sequence movements in Section 1, eg 'Can you move your tongue up to your nose and then down to your chin?' Play suggested activities in Section 1 to practise sequences of mouth movements, eg roll a dice to get a number and do mouth movements that number of times. **This is hard:** Keep working on single movements using a mirror.
Listening games	To help the child hear the speech sound **s**. To help the child hear that **s** and **t** or **s** and **d** are different speech sounds.	**Section 2:** 1. Listening activities in Section 2, eg 'Listen, when you hear me say **s**, put a seal in the sea.' 2. Play listening games from the list of games in Section 9 using **s** and other speech sounds, eg Bowling (stick **s** on one skittle and another speech sound on the other; see the list of speech sounds and the ages most children start to say them on p.1), Catch a picture, Listen and colour. 3. Play a listening game with the colouring activity in Section 2, eg 'When I say **s**, colour in a ring'.	**This is easy:** Play the variation of this listening activity in Section 2 (listen to more speech sounds and put a seal in the sea when you hear **s**, eg **m, k, p, w, s**). Use more than two speech sounds in activities, eg put **s, p, t** on skittles. Make sure the speech sounds you use in games are very different to make it easier for the child to hear **s**, eg **w, t, b, s**. **This is hard:** Play the listening games with a toy or puppet so that the child can watch and listen.

What?	Why?	How?	Next step?
Speaking games	To help the child say the speech sound **s**	**Section 2:** 1. Use a mirror so that the child can see your mouth and his mouth, eg 'Put a seal in the sea or a sausage in a saucepan or Sam on a surfboard and say **s**.' Take turns to say **s** in this activity. 2. Use the drawing activities in Section 2 to practise saying **s**, eg 'Say **s** and draw an eye on the alien'. 3. Use **s** and other speech sounds in speaking games on the list of games in Section 9, eg Kim's game (present at least three speech sounds, eg **t**, **s**, **b**; the child closes his eyes and you take away one), Pairs, Which picture?	**This is easy:** Start working on words that begin with **s** in Section 3 (**sea, Si, Sue, soy, sow, saw, say, sew**). **This is hard:** 1. See tips on helping children to say **s** (38–39). 2. Do mouth movements to help the child learn about his mouth. 3. Play listening games so that the child has lots of opportunities to hear **s** but does not feel any pressure to try to say **s**.

2. To help the child say s at the beginning of words – Section 1 and Section 3

What?	Why?	How?	Next step?
Mouth exercises	To help the child learn about his mouth and movements we make for speech.	**Section 1:** 1. Look in a mirror, eg 'Show me your tongue. Show me your teeth.' 2. Do single movements together with a mirror, eg 'Can you put your tongue up to your nose?'	**This is easy:** Sequence movements in Section 1, eg 'Can you put your tongue up to your nose and then down to your chin?' Play suggested games in Section 1 to practise sequences of mouth movements. **This is hard:** Keep working on single movements using a mirror.
Listening games	To help the child hear the speech sound **s** in words.	**Section 3:** 1. Listening activities in Section 3, eg present at least two pictures to the child, name one of them and the child holds up the one he heard you say. With children over four and a half years of age, play the listening games where you sound words out for the child, eg **s – ea (sea)**. 2. Play listening games from the list of games in Section 9 using the words in Section 3, eg Bowling, Catch a picture, Listen and colour. 3. Read the jingles from Section 3 to the child.	**This is easy:** Play listening games from Section 4. **This is hard:** Play the listening games with a toy or puppet so that the child can watch and listen. Go back to playing listening games with **s**, and with **s** and other speech sounds, so that the child has more opportunities to hear the sounds before you work on **s** in words.

What?	Why?	How?	Next step?
Speaking games	To help the child say the speech sound **s** in words.	**Section 3:** 1. Play speaking games from Section 3, eg What's the picture? Hide Sam, Roll and say. 2. Play speaking games from the list of games in Section 9 using the words from Section 3. 3. See tips at the end of Section 3 on using jingles as speaking activities, eg leaving a word out of a line of a jingle for the child to say.	**This is easy:** Start working on words that begin with **s** in Section 4. **This is hard:** See tips in Section 3 for help. Go back to working on Section 2 and gradually introduce words and games from Section 3.

3. To help the child say s at the beginning of longer words – Section 1 and Section 4

Tip Some children find it easier to say **s** at the end of a word than at the beginning. If the child you are working with finds it easier to say **s** at the ends of words, work on words from Section 5 before you work on words from Section 4.

What?	Why?	How?	Next step?
Mouth exercises	To help the child learn about his mouth and movements we make for speech. To warm up before starting work on saying **s** in words.	**Section 1:** Sequence mouth movements. Play mouth movement games from Section 1.	**This is easy:** Tell the child you are warming up before the hard work begins like footballers and athletes do before a game or race! Keep this section short and fun. **This is hard:** Keep working on single movements using a mirror.
Listening games	To help the child hear the speech sound **s** in words.	**Section 4:** 1. Listening activities in Section 4, eg Listen and guess. With children over four and a half years of age, play the listening games where you sound words out for the child, eg **s – ea (sea)**. 2. Play listening games from the list of games in Section 9 using the words in Section 4, eg Goal! 3. Read the jingles from Section 4 to the child. See tips on using the jingles at the end of Section 3.	**This is easy:** Play listening games from Section 5. **This is hard:** Play the listening games with a toy or puppet so that the child can watch and listen. Go back to Section 3.

What?	Why?	How?	Next step?
Speaking games	To help the child say the speech sound **s** in words.	**Section 4:** 1. Play speaking games from Section 4, eg Roll and say, What's the word? 2. Play speaking games from the list of games in Section 9 using the words from Section 4, eg Guess what? 3. See tips on using jingles as speaking activities at the end of Section 3, eg leaving a word out of a line of a jingle for the child to say.	**This is easy:** Start working on words that end with **s** in Section 5, eg **house**, **horse**, **juice**. **This is hard:** See tips in Section 4 for help. Go back to working on Section 3 and gradually introduce words and games from Section 4.

4. To help the child say s at the end of words – Section 1 and Section 5

What?	Why?	How?	Next step?
Mouth exercises	To help the child learn about his mouth and movements we make for speech. To warm up before starting work on saying **s** in words.	**Section 1:** Sequence mouth movements. Play mouth movement games from Section 1.	**This is easy:** Tell the child you are warming up before the hard work begins like footballers and athletes do before a game or a race! Keep this section short and fun. **This is hard:** Keep working on single movements using a mirror.
Listening games	To help the child hear **s** in words.	**Section 5:** 1. Listening activities in Section 5, eg Listen and guess. With children over four and a half years of age, play the listening games where you sound words out for the child, eg **mou – se**. 2. Play listening games from the list of games in Section 9 using the words in Section 5, eg What is it?, Catch a picture. 3. Read the jingles from Section 5 to the child. See tips on reading the jingles at the end of Section 3.	**This is easy:** Play listening games from Section 5. Use the words from Section 5 and play listening games from earlier sections. **This is hard:** Play the listening games with a toy or puppet so that the child can watch and listen. Go back to working on Section 4 and gradually introduce words from Section 5.

What?	Why?	How?	Next step?
Speaking games	To help the child say the speech sound **s** in words.	**Section 5:** 1. Play speaking games from Section 5, eg Roll and say, What's the word? 2. Play speaking games from the list of games in Section 9 using the words from Section 5, eg Kim's game. 3. See tips on using jingles as speaking activities at the end of Section 3, eg leaving a word out of a line of a jingle for the child to say.	**This is easy:** Start working on Section 6. **This is hard:** See tips in Section 5 for help. Go back to working on Section 4 and gradually introduce words and games from Section 5.

5. To help the child say s in words with more than one syllable – Section 1 and Sections 6 and 7

What?	Why?	How?	Next step?
Mouth exercises	To help the child learn about his mouth and movements we make for speech. To warm up before starting work on saying **s** in words.	**Section 1:** Sequence mouth movements. Play mouth movement games from Section 1.	**This is easy:** Tell the child you are warming up before the hard work begins like footballers and athletes do before a game or a race! Keep this section short and fun. **This is hard:** Keep working on single movements using a mirror.
Listening games	To help the child hear **s** in words.	**Section 6:** 1. Listening activities in Section 6, eg What did I say? 2. Play listening games from the list of games in Section 9 using the words in Section 6. 3. Read the jingles from Section 6 to the child. See tips on reading the jingles at the end of Section 3.	**This is easy:** Great! The child can hear the speech sound **s** at the beginning and end of words. **This is hard:** Play the listening games with a toy or puppet so that the child can watch and listen. Go back to Section 5 and gradually introduce words from Section 6.

What?	Why?	How?	Next step?
Speaking games	To help the child say the speech sound s in words.	**Section 6:** 1. Play speaking games from Section 6, eg Finish my word. 2. Play speaking games from the list of games in Section 9 using the words from Section 6. 3. See tips on using jingles as speaking activities at the end of Section 3, eg leaving a word out of a line of a jingle for the child to say.	**This is easy:** Start using words from the sections you have covered in phrases and sentences in Section 7. **This is hard:** See tips in Section 6 for help. Go back to working on Sections 5 and 4 and gradually introduce words and games from Section 6.

6. To help the child say s in words in phrases and sentences – Section 8

What?	Why?	How?	Next step?
Using words that the child has worked on in the book in phrases and sentences in games and activities.	To help the child say the speech sound s in his talking.	See tips in Section 8 for using activities, eg how to choose words to work on. Play games little and often, eg play a game from Section 8 at least three times a week.	**This is easy:** Play games in groups, not just one-to-one with the child. Give activities to carers to play at home. **This is hard:** Play games one-to-one. Keep playing games that are familiar to the child from the list of games in Section 9.

SECTION 11

IDEAS FOR WORKING ON WORDS THAT CONTAIN S

Section 11: Ideas for working on words that contain s

What next?

Make a list of words that contain the speech sound **s**. Choose words that are meaningful and useful for the child, for example, names of friends, family, teachers, peers, pets, local towns, villages and cities, places they have been on holiday, television programmes, food. Use curriculum key words so that the child has more opportunities to hear these words and to try to use them. For example:

- **Ancient Egypt:** papyrus, Isis, sphinx, goddess, desert, crops, Ra God of the sun, hieroglyphics.

- **Titanic:** sea, sink, iceberg, first class, second class, rescue.

- **Castles:** fortress, Battle of Hastings, Windsor Castle, defence.

- **Changing state:** ice, solid, water cycle, gas, solidify, condense.

Work on five to ten words a session. Rotate lists so that children don't get bored with always working on the same words. Make a word book, bag or box.

Try to work on words little and often, for example before lunch on a Wednesday, after break on a Friday.

Suggested session:

- Take it in turns to take a word out of the bag or box. Say each word for the child, so that she can hear the word.

- Ask the child to say the word after you. Aim for the best production she can do. Help her if she finds it hard by breaking words into chunks (see tips on saying longer words and on saying **s** at the end of wordsfor advice and examples). Try breaking words into syllables, eg **pa – py – rus**. Try starting at the end of the word, eg **rus – pyrus – papyrus**. Keep this activity short.

Tips

- Ask the child to imagine saying the word before she tries to say it out loud.

- Ask the child to say the word to herself quietly at least three times and then say it out loud to you.

- Put a rhythm on longer words – tap them with your finger, or nod your head as you say them, or do bigger movements, eg bend your knees on each syllable.

- Choose one or two activities or games from this book to practise saying words.

- When the child can say her words accurately at least 70 per cent of the time, add some more words. Keep a checklist of the words so that you can see progress.

- Review words regularly by taking a few out of the word bag or box and playing games and activities from this book.

- When the child is making good progress with the words, give her opportunities to use them in the nursery or classroom, eg using names that contain **s**, talking about the topic that the words are from.

- Choose a word of the day, which the child tries to say as often as she can throughout the day (encourage the child to say the word by giving her a reward, eg a sticker, a star, a marble in a jar, each time she says it).

- Make up stories and rhymes using the words. Write and illustrate them with the child in a 'Playing with s' book.

- Highlight words that contain **s** in books when you are reading with the child. For example: point them out; underline them; use a highlighter pen to raise the child's awareness of **s** in words; see who can find two words with **s** in them on the page.

- Have a one-minute challenge! The child talks about a topic of interest, or her weekend, holiday, etc. for a minute. She has to try really hard to say **s** accurately in words during the minute. Gradually increase the time, eg a two-minute challenge, a three-minute challenge. This is to help the child monitor her talking and correct errors such as saying **t** instead of **s** in words.

SECTION 12

WORD LIST

Section 3

Saw
Si (short for Simon)
Sow (female pig)
Sew
Sue
Soy (soy sauce)
Sea
Say
See-saw
Sam
Seal
Say
Swimming
Cereal
Sandwich

Section 4

Safe
Seed
Seal
Sing
Save
Sack
Sun
Seat
Sam
Soap
Soup
Sid
Sword
Sock
Sail
Suit
Sum
Sad
Sell
Sip
Song
Silly
Silliest
Some
Seb (short for Sebastian)
Singing
Sit

Section 5

Moose
Dice
Face
Dress
Bus
Boss
House
Goose
Juice
Rice
Horse
Dance
Miss
Less
Kiss
Case
Plus
Six
Purse
Mouse
Nurse
Ice
Pass
Yourself
Chase
Faster
Race

Section 6

Sandal
Sardine
Soldier
Surgeon
Princess
Seagull
Minus
Seven
Delicious
Police
Santa
Dangerous
Surfboard
Sunny
Salad
City
Seaweed
Salt

Cinema
Sausage
Saddle
Sofa
Cereal
Sandwich
Furious
Waitress
Saucepan
Tennis
Scissors
Curious
Sixteen
Sixty
Sailor
Seventeen
Seventy
Circle
Octopus
Sauce
Singer
Necklace
Sister
Sally
Yesterday
Serious
Silly
Message
Massage
Lesson
Lettuce

Section 7

Parcel
Message
Person
Dinosaur
Muscle
Icing
Lesson
Answer
Messy
Bicycle
Classroom
Pasta
Bracelet
Biscuit
Question

Icicle
Castle
Listen
Mr
Mrs

Section 8

Small
Thirsty
Sad
Scared
Excited
Surprised
Voice
Ambulance
Medicine
Hospital
Sold
Sat
Sent
Said
Asked
Sang
Sailed
Saw
Swam
Saved
Persuaded
Sacked
Upset
Searched
Seemed
Seized
Selected
Separated
Sobbed

Sorted
Celebrated
Massive
Sad
Soggy
Furious
Curious
Delicious
Marvellous
Fantastic
Fabulous
Dangerous
Soft
Similar
Safe
Same
Salty
Selfish
Sensible
Silly
Serious
Sick
Silent
Simple
Soppy
Tasty
Mr Sew
Mrs Sew
Master Sew
Miss Sew
Mr Send
Mrs Send
Master Send
Miss Send
Mr Sing
Mrs Sing

Master Sing
Miss Sing
Mr Price
Mrs Price
Master Price
Miss Price
Mr Seal
Mrs Seal
Master Seal
Miss Seal
Mr Sum
Mrs Sum
Master Sum
Miss Sum
Mr Siren
Mrs Siren
Master Siren
Miss Siren
Mr Muscle
Mrs Muscle
Master Muscle
Miss Muscle
Mr Messy
Mrs Messy
Master Messy
Miss Messy
Mr Cement
Mrs Cement
Master Cement
Miss Cement

Section 9

Sword
Sip
Sleigh

References

Flynn L & Lancaster G (1996) *Children's Phonology Sourcebook*, Speechmark Publishing, Milton Keynes.

Grunwell P (1987) *Clinical Phonology*, 2nd edn, Croom Helm, London.

Knowles W & Masidlover M (1982) *The Derbyshire Language Scheme*, Medoc Computers, Nottingham.

Ripley K, Daines B & Barrett J (1997) *Dyspraxia: a Guide for Teachers and Parents*, David Fulton Publishers, London.

Stackhouse J (1992) 'Promoting reading and spelling skills through speech therapy', Fletcher P & Hall D (eds) *Specific Speech and Language Disorders in Children*, Whurr Publishers, London.